METHODS FOR ACTIVE PARTICIPATION

Experiences in Rural Development
from East and Central Africa

Terry D. Bergdall

Nairobi
Oxford University Press
1993

Oxford University Press
Oxford New York Toronto
Delhi Bombay Calcutta Madras Karachi
Kuala Lumpur Singapore Hong Kong Tokyo
Nairobi Dar es Salaam Cape Town
Melbourne Auckland Madrid
and associated companies in
Berlin Ibadan

Oxford is a trade mark of Oxford University Press

ISBN 0 19 572785 1

Published by Oxford University Press, Eastern Africa, ABC Place,
Waiyaki Way, P.O. Box 72532, Nairobi Kenya and printed by
English Press Ltd., P.O. Box 30127, Enterprise Road, Nairobi, Kenya.

CONTENTS

PART ONE: THE DEVELOPMENT OF MAP METHODOLOGY

PART TWO: THE MAP FACILITATOR'S HANDBOOK

INTRODUCTION

The "Method for Active Participation Research and Development Project" (MAP) was initiated by the Swedish Cooperative Centre (SCC) with funding from the Swedish International Development Authority (SIDA) for work in Kenya, Tanzania, and Zambia from 1988 to 1991.

The MAP Project had four objectives: 1) to develop methodologies for promoting the participation of members in local cooperatives, 2) to assist national institutions in applying these methods, especially in the training of facilitators, 3) to develop new techniques for monitoring and evaluating participation, and 4) to make adaptations of participatory methodology for use in other development contexts outside the cooperative sector.

This volume, "Methods for Active Participation," comprises the first two parts of the final report from the MAP Project. Part One is a comprehensive review of findings from three years of field work from the project. The first chapter reviews the different historical approaches that have evolved in rural participation while the second chapter introduces MAP methodology.

The next three chapters report on the practical experimentation that has occurred with MAP in different rural development settings. These are the "Cooperative Members' Participation Programme" (CMPP) in Kenya, Zambia, and Tanzania; the "Babati Land Management Programme" (LAMP) in Tanzania; and the "Integrated Rural Development Programme" in the Eastern Province of Zambia (IRDP/EP).

The sixth chapter concerns monitoring and evaluating participation programmes. It examines problems of this type of evaluation and shares the techniques used by the MAP Project in two Tanzanian villages. The seventh chapter compares MAP with other well know participation approaches in rural development. The eighth chapter discusses other possible applications of MAP beyond the realm of rural development.

Chapter 9 examines the issue of training field facilitators. Chapter 10 is a summary and conclusion of the research project.

Part Two, "The MAP Facilitators' Handbook," is a practical guide to the participatory techniques developed by the MAP project. It is written in a simple style to describe the MAP approach thereby serving as a practical resource for the training of potential facilitators. It has also been published independently by the Cooperative Printing Press in Lusaka. Chapter 11 is an introduction to the MAP project and the role of facilitators. Though it repeats material in earlier chapters of this book, it has been included because it will assist those readers who may be primarily interested in the practical application of MAP methods.

Chapter 12 concerns techniques for enabling active participation while Chapter 13 focuses on establishing a participatory environment for conducting promotional programmes. The final chapter presents ways of ensuring quality planning in participation events.

Part Three of the MAP final report, "The MAP Manual for Training Facilitators," is a direct companion to the "Facilitators, Handbook" and consists of curriculum ideas for training animators in promoting rural participation. Though these ideas are introduced in Chapter 9 of this book, the manual itself is not included in this volume and has been published separately.

ACKNOWLEDGEMENTS

This book is a result of four years of work with the "Method for Active Participation Research and Development Project" (MAP). Many people have been involved with the MAP Project in one form or another during that period of time.

The study would have been impossible without the assistance of those institutions that have developed the "Cooperative Members' Participation Programme" (CMPP): the Cooperative College of Zambia, the Cooperative Union of Tanzania, and the Kenya National Federation of Cooperatives. The many individuals who have been involved with CMPP have all directly or indirectly contributed to the findings presented in this book and their valuable insights are gratefully acknowledged. This includes facilitators, union and ministry officials, and the enthusiastic members of the primary societies who have hosted the programme. Particular appreciation is extended to those who have served as coordinators of these national programmes: Ms J. Mapulanga, Ms B. Svensson-Thackray, and Mr D. Chimanga of Zambia; Mr M. Towo and Ms A.B. Omari of Tanzania; and Ms C. Gathuthi and Mr A. Karanja of Kenya.

Mr C.A. Gerden and Mr Mnyanga of the "Babati Land Management Programme" in Tanzania were both energetic supporters of MAP during its work in Babati. Mr D. Skoog of the SIDA office in Dar-es-Salaam opened the doors that initially allowed MAP to work the LAMP programme. A dedicated team of facilitators from Babati was also crucial to the success of the MAP activities in that district. Ms Z. Mnubi in particular assisted me with the extensive evaluation and monitoring activities in the villages of Managhat and Endabeg.

Several individuals were associated with MAP involvement with the "Integrated Rural Development Programme" in the Eastern Province of Zambia (IRDP/EP). Mr A. Yliverronen and Ms I. Rooke assisted MAP in the formation of experimental activities in the Chama and Chipata Districts along with the Programme Coordinator, Dr H. Hedlund. Mr C. Chapeshamano worked with me in evaluating the IRDP participation activities in the Chama District.

The Swedish International Development Authority (SIDA) has provided crucial funding for The Swedish Cooperative Centre (SCC) to support the work of the MAP project. Mr B. Genberg and Mr K. Fogelstorm have been staunch supporters of MAP in their capacity as Director and Acting Director of SCC. Mr B. Adelstahl, Mr L. Sylvan, and Ms B. Thackray have ably served as the project officers for MAP in Stockholm. The Zambia Cooperative Federation (ZCF) has provided an institutional home for the MAP project for the past four years.

The works of those who have been involved in past CMPP evaluations have been especially valuable to the present study. Appreciation is expressed to V. Rutachokozibwa, Z.S.K. Mvena, A.Z. Mattee, D. Noppen, M. Fuglesang, C. Lwoga, J. Eklof, and K.J.B. Keregero for work in Tanzania; M.C. Milimo, J.I. Uitto, O. Saasa, and G. Goransson in Zambia; and P.O. Alila and J.H. Obaso in Kenya. Mr J. Silvey and Mr H. McClintock of Nottingham University in England have provided me with great assistance in my own personal work in evaluating participation promotion programmes in Tanzania.

Mr U. Herath of the International Cooperative Alliance (Regional Office in Asia) provided a unique opportunity for the MAP project to reflect upon its work by inviting me to serve as the primary resource person for an Asian conference on members' participation in 1989. His subsequent work in developing practical material for use in Asia has provided a helpful dialogue for creating similar materials in Africa.

The Institute of Cultural Affairs (ICA) has been involved in the development of CMPP since it emerged and grew from its own pioneering work in Kenya. National facilitators of the ICA in Kenya and Zambia have been directly involved in field implementation activities at different stages of the MAP project. The entire team of the "intercontinental support personnel" in Nairobi was an indispensable source of intellectual stimulation and collegiality as I undertook MAP activities within the framework of "ICA restructuring." Mr R. Alton of Brussels has especially followed the development of CMPP over the years and provided valuable reflections and encouragement on the development of its methodology.

Ms Dorothy Holi patiently assisted me in preparing the illustrations found in the second part of this book. Dr Goran Hyden, Professor of Political Science at Florida State University, has graciously taken time from his busy visits to east and central Africa to meet with me and comment on my work with MAP. Dr Hans Hedlund, Coordinator of the Integrated Rural Development Project in the Eastern Province of Zambia and my former colleague in the MAP Project, has continued to provide me with practical encouragement and valuable reflections on the topic of participation.

Finally, I am grateful for the insights and reflections of my wife, Pamela, who is also a seasoned campaigner in transforming the high ideals of participation rhetoric into effective practices.

Though the input from all of the above has been deeply appreciated, the responsibility for the contents of this book remain strictly with myself. The conclusions reached do not necessary coincide with those of the Swedish Cooperative Centre or its partner organisations.

Terry D. Bergdall
Lusaka, February 1992

PART ONE: THE DEVELOPMENT
OF MAP METHODOLOGY

Chapter 1

A HISTORICAL OVERVIEW OF THE
PROMOTION OF PARTICIPATION

People's participation in rural development is a popular theme in development circles. Very few development programmes would today fail to claim some emphasis for encouraging local participation. This was amply demonstrated in Arusha, Tanzania,at the "International Conference on Popular Participation in the Recovery and Development Process in Africa." Organised by the UN Economic Commission for Africa, the conference brought together a delegation of over five hundred people composed of academics, government officials, donor administrators, and NGO practitioners during the week of 12-16 February 1990.   They were assembled to explore all aspects of participation in African development. Yet for all its theoretical popularity, even fervent advocates readily confess that "participation" often remains elusive in the realm of practice.

The Arusha conference was representative of contemporary discussions about participation and confirmed that participation means many things to many people. To some of the delegates, the theme of participation was a springboard into the politically hot debates which are presently sweeping the continent about multi-party democracy. To others, participation was one more platform for forcing reconsideration of the structural adjustment programmes of the International Monetary Fund (IMF) and the World Bank (ICPP, "African Charter for Popular Participation").

If such themes reflected an interest in the macro issues of participation in political and economic life, other delegates were more oriented to participation matters in a micro perspective. They spoke of participation issues in practical terms like people's involvement in different phases of project cycles, promotional strategies for increased participation, replicable methodologies, training of animators, approaches to evaluation and programme design.

Multifaceted ideas are obviously associated with participation even when the field has been narrowed to the concerns of rural development. In 1984, the International Labour Office (ILO) published a survey of different participatory approaches found in rural development activities and offered a sampling of definitions and statements used to describe the concept of participation; they are illustrative of a wide range of interpretations.

(a) Participation is considered a **voluntary contribution** by the people to one or another of the public programmes supposed to contribute to national development but the people are not expected to take part in shaping the programme or criticising its content.

(b) participation means...in its broadest sense, to **sensitise** people and, thus, to increase the receptivity and ability of rural people to **respond** to development programmes, as well as to encourage local initiatives.

(c) With regard to rural development...participation includes people's involvement in **decision-making** processes, in **implementing programmes**...their sharing in the **benefits** of development programmes, and their involvement in efforts to **evaluate** such programmes.

(d) Popular participation in development should be broadly understood as the **active** involvement of people in the decision-making process in so far as it affects them.

(e) Community involvement means that people, who have both the **right** and the **duty** to participate in solving their own health problems, have greater responsibilities in assessing the health needs, mobilising local resources and suggesting new solutions, as well as creating and maintaining local organisations.

(f) Participation is considered to be an **active** process, meaning that the person or group in question takes **initiatives** and asserts his/her or its autonomy to do so.

(g) ...the organised efforts to increase **control** over resources and

> regulative institutions in given social situations, on the part of groups and movements of those hitherto excluded from such control. (Oakley and Marsden, p.18)

These statements provide a glimpse of the many conflicting values and perspectives within current discussions about participation. A wide chasm undeniably separates notions that have to do with sensitizing others to "respond" from those that call for initiatives by people themselves to increase their "control" over development affairs.

This chapter offers a brief historical overview of theory and practice concerning participation. It begins with an examination of impediments to participation in Africa. This is followed by a review of three traditional approaches to promoting rural participation, including different criticisms that have been levelled against all three over the years. The third section examines the call for alternative thinking in response to these traditional approaches and then concludes with some general observations on the subject of "empowerment."

Obstacles to Rural Participation

There exists in Africa a strong tradition of centralised planning and administrative control. This is understandable in the light of the history of post-independence Africa. As observers have noted, the forging of a single national identity from different ethnic, religious, and tribal backgrounds was an overriding priority for young governments (Stiefel and Racelis). The prospect of independent power centres was usually perceived as a threat to central authority—and by extension, national unity—and was aggressively discouraged.

Centralised authority has matured into an established way of life. Even most "decentralisation" plans have merely shifted authority to surrogate administrators located in provinces or regions. The slightest sign of independence or autonomy is often dealt with quickly and harshly. Cooperatives in Tanzania were completely dissolved by the government from 1976 to 1982. One of the participation programmes reviewed in this report was suspended by the Kenyan government for three full years. It is not surprising that an attitude has emerged whereby rural people believe that the lead in development activities should be taken by recognised authorities.

Correspondingly, an atmosphere of passivity and dependence prevails in rural communities. Local initiative, when taken at all, has evolved in to a dismal shadow of its true potential. People have become accustomed to petitioning those in authority, or donors with outside resources, to do something on their behalf. They reinforce a self-perception of themselves as submissive objects of development rather than active players. The result is predictable: with a shrug of the shoulders, many villagers spend a lot of time waiting for development to happen through the efforts of others and point accusing fingers when it doesn't take place.

Some political authorities, of course, do teach the need for self-reliance and thereby give at least some rhetorical encouragement for local participation. This often takes the practical form of half measures, of enlisting people to supply labour or make financial contributions to projects that have already been decided elsewhere. The self-help tradition of *harambee* in Kenya has been so exploited.

Many attempts at locally initiated rural development projects unfortunately fail. Rural people often have limited organisational and managerial skills. This not only makes them vulnerable to intentional mismanagement and theft, but also causes projects to fail due to inadequate planning. Self-help projects are easily frustrated because of inability to analyze problems and formulate simple solutions. When such failures occur, the negative experience goes a long way to discourage similar initiatives in the future.

Women are consistently left on the fringes of most development activities. Though women supply the bulk of labour when local projects require it, they have minimal access to information, education opportunities, or decision-making. This is particularly tragic because women, as caretakers of rural families, are extremely practical. They can bring much needed-common sense to project planning but are usually excluded from the process.

There are indeed substantial impediments to broad participation in rural development. Different approaches for promoting participation have all had to contend with these obstacles. As the following reviews show, however, they have done so with varying degrees of success.

Three Traditional Approaches

It can be argued that there are nearly as many different approaches to participation as there are rural development programmes. Almost all can point to some unique characteristics that distinguish it from others. Yet, broadly speaking three traditional approaches to rural participation can be viewed: 1) the formation of agricultural cooperatives, 2) the instigation of community development activities, and 3) the inclusion, in some degree or another, of local participation in the undertaking of major development projects.

Peoples' Organisations and Cooperatives

There are several historical antecedents to the subject of rural participation. Many of them, like populist political movements and organisational activities with the urban poor, have their roots in the industrial revolution of nineteenth century Europe (Midgley, et al.). The wide-spread effort to form "people's organisations," such as trade unions and farmers,unions, have largely been borrowed from abroad and transplanted wholesale into the arena of African development. The formation of rural cooperatives has been one of the most prevalent organisational transplants to occur throughout rural Africa.

Cooperatives are conceived as voluntary associations where people organise together in order to mobilise the potential of their collective power. The intention is to establish democratically controlled structures whereby people can profit from economies of scale. Co-ops, especially through their apex organisations, are also intended to serve as a mechanism for increasing the voice of rural people in political discourse. Given the guiding principals of cooperatives, the definition and organisational structures themselves are sometimes offered as verification of their participatory nature.

The 1960s saw a rapid growth of cooperatives within the rural areas of developing countries. In the first year of Zambia's independence, the number of registered primary societies in the country grew from 220 to 1,069 with over a thousand additional unprocessed applications (Lombard, p. 20). The growth of cooperatives was similar in most African nations. This explosion in numbers mirrored the towering expectations that were held for cooperatives in the early days of independence. The actual experience over the past 30 years has fallen far short of these expectations. The resulting disillusionment is instructive to present considerations about participation.

- Local cooperative societies have been formed more on the basis of strong top-down sponsorship by the state than on local recognition of potential benefits from collective action.

- Stringent government legislation and administration has resulted in a very high degree of state control.

- Services offered by cooperatives are often inefficient and are not oriented to ordinary members or are provided in such a manner that they only benefit larger, better-off farmers.

- Malpractice, complemented by unqualified management, have resulted in very low efficiency of cooperative enterprises.

The need for rural people to organise in order to strengthen their position in society is obvious. Cooperatives are merely one form of doing so, though they are also one of the most common forms. Sustaining many of the problems associated with cooperatives is the pervasive issue of external sponsorship, especially government sponsorship. Simple logic leads one to conclude that people's organisations will be much more successful if they emerge from below rather than being imposed from above. The complexities of promoting and nurturing the natural evolution of such organisations are, however, enormous. Because of negative experiences with formal cooperative structures, some authors seek to make a clear distinction between "pseudo-cooperatives" formally registered under legislative acts and informal associations of "cooperation" with their potential for "process extension and movement building" (Verhagen,1984).

Community Development

Another important step in the evolution of participatory approaches in rural development has been the experience of "community development" and **animation rurale**. This general approach has its roots in colonial times, community development emerging from English-administered areas and **animation rurale** from those administered by the French. Because of the scarcity of government resources, it was asserted that development at the local level had to be addressed and solved by local communities themselves with the state providing very limited capital assistance and external expertise. Perhaps the biggest difference between community development as influenced by the British and the French oriented **animation rurale** was in the selection and training of "animators," i.e. those people responsible for the catalysts of community action. The community development approach recruited these workers from the nation at large and sent them to villages as outside extension officers while **animation rurale** recruited and trained young people who worked in their own home villages.

The community development approach has been widely used by governments in Asia and Africa since independence., Many of the basic features of community development (e.g. emphasis upon animators, self-reliant project planning and implementation) have also been broadly adapted by non-governmental organisations (NGOs) as a strategy of community-based development. Most contemporary activities focused on participation have either built upon the foundations of community development or have reacted against them. Either way, community development has played an important role in establishing much of the agenda for discussions about participation.

The extensive criticism of the traditional approach of community development is, therefore, important:

- Community development often assumed a simple homogeneity of interests among village residents that was not a true reflection of the situation (MacPherson, p.169).

- Though the rhetoric of community development asserted a grassroots approach, it was often eroded into the mere promotion of government projects that were centrally planned by external bureaucracies (Midgley, et al., p.19).

- When projects genuinely did emerge from the initiative of local efforts, they often were not integrated into nor coordinated with larger macro-development plans and resulted in duplication and waste (Chambers, p. 102).

- By focusing on issues of fatalism and lack of self-confidence and attempting to awaken people to their potential for self-reliance, community development tended to ignore underlying causes of poverty like limited access to land and the complexity of conflicting social, economic, and political interests (Oxfam, p.1&2-3).

Participatory Partnerships in Development Projects

A third general approach to participation can be distinguished from either fostering people's organisations (e.g. cooperatives) or promoting community-based activities (e.g. community development). It is an approach that seeks to include people in the planning and implementation of large development projects which are usually externally initiated, funded, and ultimately controlled. This approach attempts to create participatory partnerships between development authorities and the rural population.

Participation in these types of project partnerships can be accomplished in several ways with varying degrees of sensitivity and finesse. Input of opinions and ideas might be collected from local people prior to project planning; this in turn is incorporated by outside officials who actually prepare project plans. Or in a more crude form, authorities might bring plans that have already been formulated externally and submit them to local people for their rudimentary comments and tacit approval. Rural populations may or may not be included in some aspect of project implementation and evaluation. Planning schemes have been created to assist administrators as they determine the degree of popular participation at different stages in a project cycle.

One such scheme lists six project stages with a graph ranging from 100% people's involvement (complete self-reliance) on the left and 100% government control (complete top-down) on the right (Birgegard 1990, p. 12). A visual image illustrating possible priorities for participation in the project is created by plotting a mark on each graph. Figure 1 opposite depicts a "community-centred approach to popular participation" while Figure 2 depicts a "government-centred approach to popular participation." Because of the propensity of rural elites to control development projects when control is turned over to the community, the author of the scheme advocates the design in Figure 2 as "preferable if first priority is given to assist the poor." This is a conclusion which raises serious questions, though this is perhaps not the place to debate the issue. The significant point is that professional planners are seen as the ones who determine levels of people's participation in these partnerships.

Some observers have labelled this a "collaboration" approach with accompanying connotations of compromise and illegitimacy (Oakley and Marsden, p. 23). Even when efforts are made to increase the active involvement of people in various dimensions of a project cycle, external authorities, be they governmental or non-governmental organisations, remain the primary driving forces.

Limitations to participation in traditional projects have been widely recognised, causing many development professionals to seek other options. Decentralisation programmes are an attempt to transfer specifically defined aspects of authority and control to District Councils or other representative bodies. But many constraints, particularly ones of financial accountability and aid administration, make this a difficult task. In any case, as observers have noted, representative bodies remain just that: participation becomes the prerogative of a privileged few who now find themselves included in a widening but nevertheless still quite small circle of decision-makers (LeCompte).

Figure 1 Community-centred Approach to Popular Participation

	100% PEOPLE (self-reliance)	100% GOVERNMENT (top-down)
1) Ranking of needs & problems	X	
2) Design of activities		X
3) Implementation		X
4) Operation and maintenance	X	
5) Control & management of funds	X	
6) Resource mobilisation		X

Figure 2   Government-centred Approach to Popular Participation

	100% PEOPLE (self-reliance)	100% GOVERNMENT (top-down)
1) Ranking of needs & problems		O
2) Design of activities	O	
3) Implementation	O	
4) Operation and maintenance		O
5) Control & management of funds		O
6) Resource mobilisation		O

Source: "People's Participation" by Lars-Erik Birgegard

General Issues with Traditional Approaches to Participation

These different approaches raise many questions. Is participation more of a "means" to development or an "end" in itself? Is it to be considered simply a cheaper, more efficient means of achieving externally determined development aims? Is participation more of a collaboration with development projects that are largely formulated outside the community? Or should participation be understood as the more aggressive initiation of action from within a community itself? What are realistic expectations for community-based activities and what coordination is required beyond any one community? Who makes basic decisions?

The justifications offered in support of participation reveal the subtle stance many people take in relation to these questions. The following list of arguments appeared in a UNICEF publication devoted exclusively to the topic of community participation:

1)   services can be provided at lower cost
2)   more can be accomplished
3)   participation leads to a sense of responsibility for the project
4)   participation guarantees that a felt need is involved
5)   participation ensures that things are done in the right way
6)   it frees the population from dependence on professionals
7)   it uses indigenous knowledge and expertise
8)   it can be a catalyst for further development efforts
9)   participation has an intrinsic value for participants
10) conscientization can occur concerning the structural causes of poverty (White, p. 20-33).

The arguments above are very typical and often repeated by advocates of participation.   The first eight points expose a major interest in the instrumentality of participation and it is this perspective that dominates the list. Robert Chambers, an esteemed observer in the study of rural development, created a similar list in one of his early publications. He writes that "values ascribed to local participation include:

•   making known local wishes
•   generating development ideas
•   providing local knowledge

- testing proposals for feasibility and improving them
- increasing the capability of communities to handle their affairs and to control and exploit their environment
- demonstrating support for a regime
- doing what government requires to be done
- extracting, developing, and investing local resources (labour, finance, managerial skills, etc.)
- promoting desirable relationships between people especially through cooperative work" (Chambers, p. 85-86).

The predominance of these strong instrumental justifications about participation has occasioned the fear, indeed the accusation, that the promotion of participation can easily slip into simple manipulation. One such indictment declares its viewpoint in its title, "Beware of Participation." It describes how the "the technocratic use of popular participation implies turning demands and hopes into instructions, into orders. The technocrat collects demands, analyses them, processes them, and translates them into a plan or programme that, in his opinion, must lead to their satisfaction; democracy is thus turned into a bureaucracy" (Esteya, p. 77).

In this view, most "mobilisation" work is understood to be a manipulative process, perhaps even a coercive process, where rural populations are intentionally kept in a passive subordinate position.

Participation and the Search for a Radical Alternative

Dissatisfaction and frustration has marked much current thought about participation. Since the 1970s, participation has been increasingly reconsidered within the framework of larger issues. Conventional development programmes, it has been argued, were essentially conceived within a broader paradigm that advocated a strategy for economic growth (Wolfe, p. 80-81). Though refinements and revisions have taken place over the years, the basic tenets of this strategy have held that investment priorities in major projects, especially in support of some form of industrialisation, would lead an entire society into a gradual but steady improvement in the standard of living. Agriculture needed to be improved and integrated into growing commercialisation efforts. Within this model, it was crucial, therefore, to mobilise the rural poor through education and extension work so that their inefficient ways could be overcome and so that they could begin to play a role in the general development process.

Major disappointments have undermined the confidence of many people in this strategy of economic growth. Alternative strategies for development have been sought for a number of reasons: the appearance of gross inequities in the distribution of resources; disruptions caused by the modernisation of economies, which have raised the prospect of large segments of society losing their means of traditional livelihood without locating a place for themselves in the new economic environment; failures to meet basic human needs (see Wisner).

This search for alternatives has often been vague and idealistic, but "people-centred" perspectives (in contrast to the old "production-centred" model) have certainly caused a renewed interest in participation (Korten and Klass, et al.). Participation has been seen in much of this alternative thinking "as a strategy for the creation of opportunities to explore new, often open-ended directions with those who were traditionally the objects of development" (Oakley and Marsden, p. 13). Participation thereby becomes much more of an "end" in itself rather than a means in support of a conventional development strategy because "participation cannot be inserted as a 'missing ingredient' into most styles of development. The style itself must change, both as a result of new forms of participation and as a condition for such participation" (UNRISD, p.17).

"Power" and "control" are two concepts which have dominated much of the participation debate since the 1970s. The United Nations Research Institute for Social Development (UNRISD) established a research programme into popular participation in 1979 and focused on understanding power and control. The director of the popular participation research programme at UNRISD called this an "empowerment approach" which has been critical of "past approaches to participation on the grounds that they:

- had evaded the issue of the power component of participation

- had been excessively project-oriented, ignoring the wider context of social structures, forces and ideologies in which projects took place, and had been excessively preoccupied with the technical and managerial aspects of participation

- had been too legalistic and had placed excessive faith and importance in formal, official institutions and organisations; and that

- whatever their intentions, they had fundamentally remained ' top-down ' approaches, considering the poorer social group as ' minors ' who had to be helped, organised and provided with external expertise, etc." (Stiefel, p. 23).

The ILO survey cited at the beginning of the chapter considers the question of power to be the essential distinction when considering matters of participation. The definitions and statements about participation which it reviewed were seen in this light. There are those statements which "inextricably equate participation with the achieving of some kind of power" and those that reflect more conventional and instrumental approaches to development (Oakley and Marsden, p.13).

Observers who make this distinction categorise particular participation activities as either "system-maintaining" or "system-transforming" (Rudqvist). They ask if a given participation activity is attempting to identify and challenge the structural causes of poverty within an economic/political system, and thereby "transform" it, or is it attempting merely to integrate people into the existing system through an "ameliorative" process of gradual improvements.

Closely linked to this perception of participation as "empowerment" and "transformation" are the ideas of Paulo Freire whose liberation writings originally introduced the influential concept of conscientization (Freire). Sometimes referred to as "awareness training", conscientization occurs through the limited intervention of outsiders who interact with people by posing problems and generating discussions, thereby awakening people to the structural causes of their poverty (Hope and Timmel). This is an educational process of discovery. Disciples of Freire avoid the traditional role of teachers and extension officers who give instruction in correct ways to think and act. All action emerging from the conscientization process should arise from the consensus of a social group itself and should draw entirely upon people's own creativity and knowledge.

Much of the "empowerment" literature regarding participation, with its radical rhetoric for transformation, ultimately advocates conflict and confrontation (Wisner, p. 46-52). This often elevates its discussions to the lofty realms of abstraction. A subtle bias exists in much of this literature against any promotional activity undertaken by outsiders for the enhancement of local participation. One such writer remarks upon the surprising "paternalism" that is even found in the conscientization work of Paulo Freire (Midgely, et al., p. 22). An echo is heard here of the idealism of the 1981 UN paper on participation that subordinates "induced" participation to that of "spontaneous" participation (UN, p. 8).

Any serious effort that involves social change will certainly cause confrontation, but dealing with conflict in practice is far different from considering it in theory. External intervention for the sake of promoting participation must almost always function in some kind of accord with established authorities. In most participatory activities, it is a very qualitative, if not subjective, distinction which must be made between transformation and amelioration. Short of revolution, participatory development programmes are almost always going to be vulnerable to charges from radical observers of being merely reformist.

It is easy to discern a difference between a question that asks from a speculative distance "how can genuine participation be recognized and distinguished from counterfeits?" and one that asks from direct involvement "how can participation be effectively promoted?" The former can afford the luxury of precise criteria and radical expectations while the latter must reconcile itself to the give and take of practical action set within the confining limits of particular institutions.

In practice, empowerment cannot be observed as a distinct approach parallel to other participatory approaches as some radical writers seem to imply. Empowering of the rural poor will only be found in promotional activities that can be described as community-based, fostering people's organisations, or project partnerships. Empowerment is an important qualitative dimension of these three approaches. Incorporating power can be a very real possibility even with the most traditional programmes of community development (MacPherson, p. 96). One researcher who has written extensively on the subject states that "**empowerment** is a key aspect of participation, but it is not the whole of participation. The challenge is how to increase the power associated with participation" (Uphoff, p. 5).

This challenge is a big one because complex factors must be carefully addressed if those "hitherto excluded" are to become agents of their own development: patterns of passivity must be broken, structural constraints must be recognised, realistic options must be found, and practical action must be collectively organised.

Severe, often valid criticism has been levelled against different aspects of traditional participation approaches. This criticism provides an ad hoc agenda for those institutions or individuals who are interested in formulating new participatory approaches for rural development. The following chapters report on the experimental work of the "Method for Active Participation Research and Development Project."

Chapter 2

MAP RESEARCH AND DEVELOPMENT

In a recently published survey of rural participation programmes, one well-known researcher has suggested that a conceptual distinction between "strategy" and "methodology" is helpful in understanding different aspects of participatory approaches (Oakley). This is true in spite of the fact that the two categories often tend to flow into one another without a sharp boundary to divide them. "Strategy" on the one hand has to do with the broad design of a programme as it strives to achieve its intended aims. External agencies organise their intervention within rural areas according to particular strategies. "Methodology" on the other hand has to do with practical techniques of interacting with people as participation programmes are implemented. A subtle distinction perhaps, but a useful one.

The research work of the "Method for Active Participation Research and Development Project" (MAP) has addressed both of these issues. Part Two of this volume focuses exclusively upon matters of participatory **methodology** and is presented as a "Handbook for MAP Facilitators." It describes in detail specific techniques that allow for effective interaction with participants. This methodology has permitted MAP to emerge as a flexible tool that can be applied in many different circumstances to enhance rural participation.

Within the actual experimental work of the MAP R&D Project, questions of **strategy** have been addressed through adaptations of methodology to meet the specific aims of particular programmes. These are described in Chapters 3 to 5. The adaptation of MAP methodology has resulted in an array of insights that will assist managers as they design participation approaches within the given framework of their programmes. These strategic insights will also benefit planners as new programmes and projects are conceived and initiated.

The present chapter is merely an introduction to MAP in regard to "strategy" and "methodology" since further elaboration on both subjects will occur later in the book. It is divided into three major sections. The first introduces MAP methodology through a brief examination of its underlying assumptions. The second section reviews some of the typical methodological elements that comprise MAP. The final section of the chapter considers issues related to strategy as revealed in the application of MAP methodology.

Underlying Assumptions of MAP Methodology

The flexibility of MAP means that it can be used in a variety of circumstances embodying diverse values and intentions. MAP methodology, however, is built upon a central underlying assumption in every situation: **rural people can be agents of their own development**. Though development is a complex process involving many factors, there is no need for villagers to wait for others to take the lead, be they government officials, academic experts, or foreign donors. Development "by the people" has a much greater potential for sustainability than development "for the people."

Short-term **seminars** can be a means to many ends: enabling new awareness among participants, building practical action plans, reinforcing patterns of effective teamwork. MAP employs a series of techniques to ensure that every participant in a planning workshop contributes ideas to the process while being encouraged to think well beyond shallow perceptions of complex problems. MAP assumes that everyone, even illiterate participants, can effectively participate in the rational process of a structured seminar when workshop techniques have been appropriately adapted.

MAP seminars are a **forum for farmers** to express their concerns, to ask their questions, make their demands, and state their desires. They also provide an opportunity for local leaders to face ordinary villagers in an open-ended "question time." The content of MAP discussions is never predefined. All ideas and suggestions in MAP seminars are recorded and eventually displayed for all to see. Every suggestion is considered and included in the overall planning scheme. This is important because it allows for all social strata within the community to advocate their interests.

In MAP seminars, **participants are treated as the experts,** i.e. as people who have gained a wealth of latent knowledge, though perhaps not technical expertise, through years of practical experience. The workshop leaders play the role of "facilitators," guiding the group through a structured process of digging insights out of their accumulated wisdom. This involves a mix of individual "brainstorming," where participants do their own solitary thinking, small team discussion, and larger group dialogue where issues are explored in great depth and a broad consensus is reached.

MAP participants **analyze problems** and **plan self-help projects.** These are complementary dynamics and one is incomplete without the other. As MAP workshops move toward having people plan projects based on locally felt needs and implemented with locally available resources, participants often realise through their own interaction with each other that many suggestions are over-ambitious and cannot be realised. Facilitators enable such conclusions to emerge from the group rather than imposing them on the basis of their own opinions.

The projects planned in MAP workshops are often small projects that people can accomplish by themselves. Through accomplishing small-scale projects villagers can gain experience in the **practical management** of organisational details like budgeting time, working together, and accounting for funds. Important organisational skills can develop slowly but substantially on a solid foundation of local project implementation. Small successes can breed confidence for bigger undertakings.

Through the interactive learning process of discussing problems, planning activities, and successfully implementing projects, participants can acquire a **new self-perception.** They begin to see themselves as agents of their own development rather than as passive victims who are merely dependent upon the generosity of others. If MAP contains an inherent aim in its methodology, it is to serve as a catalyst for enabling this new awareness and self-confidence to emerge. Rather than lecture rural people on how they "ought to think and act," MAP sets the stage for people to experience a new reality of themselves.

Basic Elements of MAP Methodology

MAP uses seminars as its primary means for promoting participation. The precise content of these seminars is determined by the particular aims and objects of the programme utilising the MAP methods. These often vary considerably from one another as the examples found in the following chapters clearly illustrate. For the sake of introducing MAP, however, it is useful to review some of the most typical features found in MAP planning seminars.

A MAP seminar is usually a two-day planning event. It is attended by a representative group of people chosen according to criteria established by the particular programme. Most often 30 to 40 participants are invited to attend.

MAP seminars typically consists of five "workshops." The seminar begins with the **Vision Workshop** where the question under consideration is "what do you hope to see five years ahead as a result of this programme's activity?" Participants share their ideas in small teams. These teams then report, creating a list of vision elements which are prioritised by the whole group. This procedure of individual "brainstorming," small team discussion, and large group consensus usually takes place in all of the workshops.

There is a continual interplay in MAP workshops between discussions in small teams, which number no more than 15 people, and the larger reporting sessions, or "plenaries," where team conclusions are presented to the whole group. This allows everyone to contribute ideas, even those who might be too shy to speak in front of large groups. This interplay with the small groups is particularly important for women who are traditionally expected to sit silently in large meetings while men do the speaking.

In the **Obstacles Workshop** participants divide into teams to consider "why have these vision elements not been realised?" Each team determines lists of the most important obstacles. Reassembled as a whole group, the teams usually report once again the results of their deliberations. The facilitators then lead a group discussion as to why the problems have not been solved until the group gains a deeper understanding about the real problems. This session is often the most intense in MAP seminars because long-held grievances are finally given a chance for a public airing. For women it is often a first opportunity to ask their questions and to receive significant information about local development activities.

The workshop on obstacles is followed by a brief discussion on **Proposals**: "What can the people in this area do to solve these problems?" This workshop usually brings the first day of the seminar to an end.

The second day of a MAP seminar often shifts the focus of discussion to creating village **Self-help Projects**. Small teams suggest specific projects they deem important in the light of the previous discussions. Reassembled, the teams report to each other and then select and schedule projects for the coming year.

The seminar ends with an **Implementation Workshop** where an anticipated accomplishment is named for the first scheduled project, key implementation steps are identified, and two coordinators for each project are selected by the group. The same procedure is followed for a special project called "Inform and Involve" village people in the plan. The purpose of this last point is to disseminate information from the seminar discussions and to open the possibility for wider involvement for people who did not attend.

Depending upon the particular design of the programme, a series of **follow-up meetings** and **monitoring visits** usually occur. After a designated period of time, a programme concludes its intervention by holding a **participatory evaluation** reviewing results and planning future activities. The nature of all this work depends entirely upon the specific aims and objectives of a programme utilising MAP methods.

Strategic Issues in the Application of MAP Methodology

If "methodology" pertains to the immediate form of interaction with participants, "strategy" has to do with the overall coordinated design of a programme for achieving intended results. Strategic options are nearly limitless when it comes to designing a participation programme. There are no universal guidelines in doing so, only variables with different values and priorities.

The preceding chapter examined many of the theoretical problems associated with participation promotion. Theoretical debates over such issues as the genuine nature of "empowerment" or participation as an end rather than a means are nearly endless. In contrast to many theoretical discussions, the strategic questions reviewed below have all emerged from the actual experiences of the MAP Project. They indicate the multiplicity of options involved in the design of participation programmes. And as can be seen, almost every strategic question has a number of different possible answers.

Centrally planned, "sectoral" projects? Many large development programmes are centrally planned with major projects already determined but hope to include some degree of community participation. This is often true of "sector specific" projects that have a particular focus and require some form of technical expertise, e.g. health, irrigation, forest conservation, etc. The degree of participation found in needs assessment and in the identification, planning, implementation, and evaluation of projects are all strategic aspects of the programme design. MAP especially confronted these issues by involving various interest groups in the planning of environmental projects in the LAMP programme in the Babati District of Tanzania.

Community-based focus? While some programmes have a sectoral emphasis, the local community residents are engaged in project planning and implementation. Often this means setting their own priorities based upon local perceptions of the particular sectoral topic of the project. On the other hand, some community-based programmes have no particular sectoral focus at all, leaving community residents totally responsible for organising themselves to plan and implement whatever projects they consider important.

Community-based participation programmes can have a vast assortment of particular aims. Some might strive to strengthen existing institutions like village governments, schools, or local cooperatives. Others might be more open-ended and endeavour to mobilise grassroots action irrespective of existing organisations. Does the programme hope to accomplish communal work on infrastructure projects that will benefit the entire community or does it desire to see personal incomes enhanced through new entrepreneurial activities? The former will probably work with all members of the community while the latter will likely form small homogeneous groups composed of peers who share interests and have a sense of mutual trust.

MAP worked with both sectoral and open-ended community-based programmes. The IRDP/EP in Zambia often sought to involve local residents in particular projects, e.g. water-well maintenance, while the CMPP in Kenya, Tanzania, and Zambia were largely open-ended with local participants setting their own priorities and determining project topics.

Provision of external inputs? Does the programme intend to assist people through the extension of favourable credit, donation of funds, contribution of materials, or provision of technical assistance? If so, on what basis? The supply of such external inputs is a major focus of many programmes promoting community-based development and self-help activities.

Other community-based programmes discourage any such provision at all. There are, of course, limitations on what very poor villagers can do solely on the basis of their own resources; people can only lift themselves so far by pulling on their "bootstraps." But a shift in self-perception, from a passive victim to an active player in development, is a realistic expectation of self-help activities. Conversely, these programmes argue, the premature introduction of external capital from a charitable patron sends the wrong message: it undermines self-confidence and reinforces a passive attitude by communicating that it does indeed pay to wait.

Women in development? Is the programme to have any special emphasis on involving rural women in development activities? If so, how? Much has been written recently on the need to "integrate" women's participation into the mainstream of development activities rather than establish programmes that "segregate" women off to themselves. Do the practical mechanisms for women's participation reflect the programme's intended aims? All of the MAP adaptation experiences have wrestled with these questions.

Intensity of the intervention? Participation programmes can vary in their geographical coverage and in their time commitment to work within a given area. Is the commitment for the short term or the long term? Is the programme designed for intensive work within a few communities or for expansive outreach activities spread across many different places?

The critical issue for a programme with a professed expansive strategy is to discern the minimal intensity of support required for achieving meaningful results. The big issue for a programme with an intensive strategy is to avoid developing a sense of dependency among participants.

Responsibilities of animators? The role of animators, or facilitators, is often a reflection of the strategic intensity of a programme. Does the animator serve as an intermédiary to help link a community with external services and resources? Do they provide technical advice and training as well as facilitating the planning process? How often does an animator visit an area? Indeed, are they recruited and trained from among community residents or are they externally placed? Are they government agents or employed by an NGO? The answers to these questions are all indications of the strategy employed by a participation programme.

The methodologies developed by the MAP Project can be effectively utilised in any of the above choices. When combined with specific strategic perspectives, methodology then becomes the practical "building blocks" for designing a participation programme. The following three chapters report on the particular programmes that have experimented with MAP methods during the past three years.

Chapter 3

COOPERATIVE MEMBERS' PARTICIPATION PROGRAMME

The Cooperative Members' Participation Programme (CMPP) has provided the primary experimental laboratory in the application of MAP methodology. CMPP has been active in the nations of Kenya, Tanzania, and Zambia where distinct economies, political structures, and cultural traditions prevail. Cooperatives also differ considerably in each country causing the national CMPPs to develop their own unique characteristics.

As one of its final activities, the MAP Project hosted the "Regional CMPP Symposium" in Harare, Zimbabwe, in August 1991. Representatives from the three national CMPPs met to share experiences and examined various methodological adaptations that have been made within the programme. This chapter presents CMPP in accordance with current operations at the time of the Symposium.

The chapter begins with a review of the background activities that preceded the launching of CMPP. Each national CMPP is then examined. The final section considers major distinguishing features that have evolved over the years within the different national programmes.

Background to the Development of CMPP

The Swedish Cooperative Centre has been one of the driving forces behind the development of CMPP. SCC, with its emphasis on strengthening cooperative movements in the developing world, is extremely clear about the many problems involved. Top-down sponsorship, stringent legislation, inefficient services, and local mismanagement all continue to frustrate cooperative development. Though strong cooperative ideals guide SCC in all its activities, a recent report from its Director pointed out that

> "in practical assistance work we are sometimes confronted with situations where the basic cooperative values, especially the issue of cooperative democracy, in too high a degree have been neglected. Our experience and conviction are that only independent, member-governed cooperative organisations can be successful in the long run" (SCC 1988-89 Annual Report, p. 5).

This conviction undergirds SCC's commitment to developing practical approaches to increasing members' involvement in the affairs of local cooperatives. Interest in reversing "neglect" in members' involvement has been the basis of SCC support in the development of CMPP.

SCC has a long history in the development of CMPP. The programme was originally created through the collaborative efforts of the Swedish Cooperative Centre, the Kenya National Federation of Cooperatives, and the Institute of Cultural Affairs (ICA). This section traces the historical development of CMPP with a brief review of the early collaboration between these three organisations.

The Institute of Cultural Affairs

The Institute of Cultural Affairs is a global network of affiliated, non-profit, non-governmental organisations in different nations that are concerned with the human factor in world development. ICA International (ICAI) serves as the world-wide coordinating body and is located in Brussels. The ICAI has Category II consultative status with the United Nations Economic and Social Council (ECOSOC) and the United Nations Children's Fund (UNICEF). It is a member of the International Council of Voluntary Agencies (ICVA) and the International Council on Social Welfare (ICSW). In Africa, the ICA is active in Kenya, Nigeria, Zambia, Cote d'Ivoire, and Egypt. The ICA also operates in dozens of other nations around the world (ICAI Annual Report, p. 2).

The major focus of the ICA during the past 25 years has been research and training in such diverse fields as education, community development, and organisational transformation. Though the ICA is not a religious organisation, it does address universal questions about ultimate significance and self-understanding in human endeavour. It asserts that effective collective action is never merely a matter of logical planning but must be set in the context of larger human concerns. Thus the reason for its name, The Institute of **Cultural** Affairs (ICA Network Exchange, p. 2).

The ICA began operations in Kenya in 1975 and a year later started the "Kawangware Human Development Project (HDP)" in an urban slum on the western edge of Nairobi. Key aspects of the Kawangware HDP were the attention given to comprehensive development and the central role of local residents. The Kawangware HDP was guided by five operating principles.

- **Work within a small, delimited geographical area.** Too large of an area renders it extremely difficult for local residents to work together in any meaningful, practical way.
- **Address all problems.** Problems are interconnected and cannot be easily isolated, be they economic, political, or social. One problem always leads to another that reinforces it.
- **Work with all the people.** People of different ages, sexes, or social status all contribute to the dynamic reality of community life. Ignoring segments of a community undermine efforts to solve problems and accomplish lasting change.
- **Address the "depth human problem."** The self-perception people have of themselves controls the way they act. If they see themselves as victims of forces beyond their control, such fatalism naturally leads to passivity.
- **Symbols are key.** Symbols maintain a subtle yet continual rehearsal of people's self-perceptions. The most catalytic forms of action are those that indirectly utilise meaningful symbolic activities (ICA 1975, p. 6).

The Kawangware HDP was created during a two-week planning event that brought together a group of 50 voluntary "consultants," i.e. government officials, academics, and businessmen, to assist residents in creating a plan for improving their community. Using a participatory approach, the ICA staff facilitated a process that enabled the mix of consultants and residents to 1) envision a positive but realistic future for the community, 2) analyze problems, 3) propose solutions, 4) create strategic directions, and 5) formulate a practical action plan for project implementation. This resulted in the creation of a master plan. The ICA staff then took up residence in Kawangware and worked as a catalyst with community residents and leaders in project implementation.

In 1979, the ICA expanded its work into rural development activities when it initiated the Kamwaleni Human Development Project in the village of Kamwaleni in the Mputi Division, Machakos District. The Kamwaleni HDP was created by ICA using a similar process to the one it used in Kawangware. From this base in Machakos, the ICA launched the New Village Movement.

With the New Village Movement (NVM) the ICA shifted its approach from intensive work in a few human development projects to an expansive strategy of replicating participatory development projects to a very large number of rural villages. By 1982, the ICA was working with 202 villages. Three strategic innovations allowed this rapid expansion to take place.

First, the planning process was abbreviated into a series of short village consultations. Second, young volunteers were recruited from areas participating in the NVM and received six weeks of training in supporting self-help ventures planned in villages. After the initial training period, the volunteers began a regular rhythm of follow-up meetings within village clusters. Because these volunteers were constantly on the road moving from one village to another, they became known as "circuiters." By 1982, 270 Kenyan circuiters were involved in NVM work. Circuiters worked in villages other than their own in order to provide an outside objectivity to the follow-up work. Third, the NVM involved the training of local village leaders in short-term courses on sustaining self-help activities (Gikonyo, Genberg and Hedlund).

The Kawangware HDP, Kamwaleni HDP, and the NVM were ICA efforts to create a participatory approach for urban and rural community development. In the late 1970s, ICA began adapting a similar approach for facilitating planning events with public and private sector organisations. These events were called "Leadership Effectiveness and New Strategies (LENS)" consultations.

LENS assisted groups within organisations who were responsible for working together in accomplishing shared tasks. These have ranged from senior management of private sector companies to the volunteer board of directors and project staff of non-governmental organisations. The number of participants in LENS seminars would range from as small a number as 10 to as many as 40. As consultants, ICA staff were responsible for facilitating planning events but then were completely uninvolved in any implementation activities. That was the sole responsibility of the client organisation.

The LENS methodology was a direct adaptation of the planning process that ICA had been using in its rural development programmes. It followed a process of small teamwork discussions and interchange which asked the group to reach a consensus on five basic questions.

1) VISION-
   what realistic hopes and dreams do participants have for their organisation?

2) CONTRADICTIONS-
   what is preventing such an envisioned future from being realised?

3)   PROPOSALS-
      how can these obstacles be overcome, by-passed, or eliminated?

4)   TACTICS-
      what practical activities must be done if these proposals are to be
      successfully accomplished?

5)   IMPLEMENTATION CALENDAR-
      what, who, when, where, and how for the next 90 days?

Whereas these were the same basic steps that constituted the planning for
the Kamwaleni and Kawangware HDPs, the LENS seminars took place in
two or three days instead of two weeks. Most importantly, they were
facilitated in a style and working environment consistent with the sophistication
of the audience.

KNFC, SCC, and ICA Collaboration Prior to CMPP

The Kenya National Federation of Cooperatives became acquainted with the
ICA in 1981 and arranged for an initial test of the LENS approach within
cooperative structures. Two LENS events were conducted by the ICA with
the Muwuti Farmers' Cooperative Society and the Changara Cooperative
Society in Bungoma District of the Western Province. Participants in
both of these seminars were management committee members, society
staff, and selected member representatives. The total number of participants in each was between 25 and 30. Later in the year, a third special
LENS seminar for women only took place in the Changara Society.

Through these activities with KNFC, the Swedish Cooperative Centre
was introduced to the ICA and also became quite interested in the possible
applications of such work for cooperatives. SCC undertook two evaluation
studies of the ICA: one of the New Village Movement in 1982 and the other
in 1983 of long-term impact resulting from the Bungoma LENS events
two years before.

From November 1983 to February 1984, KNFC and ICA carried out a
series of joint LENS seminars with five different cooperatives located in the
Nairobi area. Two of these were with consumer cooperatives, two were with
savings and credit societies, and one was with an arts cooperative.

Later in 1984, SCC agreed to fund KNFC, with the assistance of the ICA,
in conducting a pilot project of nine LENS events and follow-up meetings
with rural cooperatives in the Machakos, Murang'a, and Kirinyaga Districts.
Before the project could get underway, however, KNFC had to close its
education department due to severe financial problems. This resulted in a
request by KNFC for ICA to become the implementing agent of the pilot

project. Another agreement was reached by SCC, KNFC, and ICA in 1985 to continue the pilot project by conducting an additional nine LENS events in the same three districts.

The 1984-85 pilot project of LENS with rural cooperative societies was evaluated by SCC in February 1986 (Hedlund, 1986). The evaluation concluded that the results of the pilot project were very encouraging and reported several illustrations of how LENS had managed to instill a sense of enthusiasm and voluntary participation among both district officers and ordinary cooperative members. Based on the positive results of ICA's co-op work with LENS, the evaluation recommended that a newly named "Cooperative Members' Participation Programme" (CMPP) should be formally established, shifting the identity of the project away from the ad hoc work of the ICA and LENS into an on-going service of KNFC.

In July 1986, CMPP became fully operational at KNFC in accordance with the recommendations from the evaluation. Funding was provided by SCC. Subsequent discussions between SCC and cooperative officials in Tanzania and Zambia resulted in the organisation of international study tours to Kenya in May and June 1987 which set the stage for the launching of CMPP in those nations.

CMPP in Kenya

CMPP in Kenya began it formal activities at KNFC in July 1986 funded through "Movement to Movement" assistance from SCC. Two Kenyans were hired on a full–time basis to serve as national facilitators. One expatriate, placed by SCC, was also attached to KNFC to work with CMPP on a part-time basis. During the following twelve months, CMPP activities took place in four districts: Nyeri, Machakos, Murang'a, and Kirinyaga. District Cooperative Training Officers (DCTO) from the Ministry and Cooperative Education and Training Officers (CEPO) from the district unions were trained in facilitation methods and assisted the national facilitators in conducting CMPP activities. A total of 19 new societies were involved with CMPP through July 1987 (Alila and Obaso).

Progress stopped, however, in July 1987, when CMPP was suspended by the Ministry of Cooperative Development. The public reason given by the Ministry for this suspension was poor reporting from KNFC. Subsequent management problems at KNFC resulted in SCC withholding its financial support, causing an additional complication and delay in reactivating CMPP in Kenya. Finally in August 1990, renewed CMPP activities were allowed to take place in two primary societies to enable an extensive external evaluation. This CMPP evaluation was conducted in October and recommended a full re-initiation of the programme in 1991.

At the time of writing, however, CMPP in Kenya is still awaiting final approval from the Ministry before commencing full operations.

The following description of the CMPP methodology in Kenya is based on recommendations from this evaluation and on reports from the Kenyan delegation at the "CMPP Regional Symposium" held in Harare in August 1991.

The Implementation of CMPP in Kenya

Primary cooperative societies are central to CMPP activities in Kenya, but this focus begins in a bottom-up fashion with CMPP seminars being held in every sub-division of a primary society. These initial CMPP seminars are held in the geographical areas served by collection depots or by service centres, e.g. coffee factories.

All members of the elected management committee which governs the primary cooperative society attend a two-day planning seminar and are joined by the society's professionally employed staff. Additional representative members of the co-op are invited to attend until the number of participants reaches a total of 30 to 40. Women are encouraged to attend but no quotas are imposed.

The planning seminar begins with an abbreviated workshop on the "vision." Participants brainstorm vision items and share them in very small groups of three people. These small groups each decide upon two important vision items for the society and write each on index cards. The facilitator has all cards from all of the mini-groups passed forward where they are displayed by tape on the front wall. No effort is made to organise this information. Participants are asked to name five or six key areas of vision as overarching titles. Participants do not leave the plenary room during this workshop which is completed, from start to end, within 30 minutes.

The "obstacles" and "proposals" workshops closely follow procedures described in Part Two, "The MAP Facilitators' Handbook." Participants are arbitrarily divided into three teams where brainstorms are shared. Each team selects from 12 to 15 brainstorm items which are written on index cards and reported in the plenary session. Brainstorm items from all three teams are organised into similar categories. These categories are then named with summary titles. Both   workshops take approximately two and a half hours to complete: 45 to 60 minutes for teamwork, followed by plenary discussion of 60 minutes to organise information into categories and 30 minutes to name titles for each category. Both are done on the first day of the seminar with a break for lunch occurring between the "obstacles" and the "proposals."

The second day of the seminar begins with the "projects" workshop with procedures that differ somewhat from those of the day before. The group is divided into teams where each is assigned one or two of the major "proposal" categories. The teams discuss possible projects and conclude by choosing eight for each category. "Projects" selected are to be ones that the primary society can complete by using its own resources. In plenary session, the projects are scheduled sequentially over the next two years within broad blocks of time of approximately three months each. The workshop ends with five or six tracks of scheduled projects. These tracks are determined by the major proposal categories. The "projects" workshop usually takes two and half hours to complete with half of the time in teams and half in plenary.

After lunch, the "Implementation Workshop" takes place. Any projects which call for capital improvements are noted for referral to the society management committee who will then undertake a formal decision about how, when, or if to do the project. Projects that are strictly local self-help and require no capital investment are then considered by members residing in the geographical area of the sub-division. Teams name an anticipated accomplishment and identify four key implementation steps for each self-help project that are scheduled for the first quarter. Coordination of the projects is delegated to the co-op management committee members residing within the area. This workshop is usually completed with an hour spent in teamwork and an hour in plenary discussion.

After seminars are held in all of the sub-divisions, a concluding society-wide CMPP seminar is held. Key participants in this seminar are members of the society management committee, which is the formal elected leadership for the society. Representatives from the sub-divisions report to them on the vision, obstacles, and proposals as were discussed in all of the sub-divisions. Plans for self-help projects are reported upon and implications for the whole society are examined. The management committee then considers the different ideas for capital investments which were recommended from the sub-divisions. The seminar ends by scheduling projects they consider appropriate for the society's future.

Two follow-up meetings are conducted in each society, once after three months and then again after six months. The facilitators meet with the management committee during these follow-up meetings to review progress on the self-help projects of the sub-divisions and to review progress on the society's capital-investment projects. No other monitoring activities by the facilitators are undertaken besides these two meetings.

In the early days of CMPP in Kenya, coordinators were named for self-help projects in the sub-divisions. A few of these coordinators were then selected for special training in the managing and sustaining of self-help activities. This training was discontinued after the 1990 evaluation along with the practice of naming local coordinators for projects planned in CMPP seminars. Though management committee members were often named as project coordinators, it was felt that on those occasions when ordinary members were named as coordinators an unhelpful competition was created which challenged the officially elected leadership.

The pattern of work conducted by the facilitators in a primary society is known as the "CMPP Cycle of Activities." In summary, this looks as follows in Kenya:

CMPP Cycle of Activities in Kenya

month 1   confirmation of targeted societies in a district; set-up meeting with the union and societies

month 2   CMPP seminar with the district union
           CMPP seminar with sub-divisions of societies
           CMPP seminar with the society management committee

month 5   first follow-up with society management committee

month 8   second follow-up with society management committee.

An interesting invention in Kenya is the creation of the "policy-makers seminar." The purpose of this seminar is to introduce the concept and practice of CMPP to high ranking officials of the cooperative movement and government through a demonstration of the methodology. It is much easier to have these officials understand CMPP through experiencing an actual seminar instead of listening to an abstract explanation while sitting in an office. For two days these officials consider the vision, obstacles, and proposals to a relevant question for their work: "how can cooperatives be an effective tool for development?" This experience allows them to appreciate how and why CMPP can work when it is offered to primary societies.

CMPP seminars are also conducted with the management committees of district cooperative unions whenever CMPP is introduced into a district for the first time. In these seminars, the committee is joined by union staff and a few representative delegates from the societies as they think about the vision, obstacles, and projects for the union as a whole. Such seminars not only introduce the CMPP methodology but also become an effective planning tool for the union.

CMPP in Kenya has the ambition to have primary societies pay for expenses related to CMPP seminars.

Results of CMPP in Kenya

CMPP in Kenya was suspended by order of the Ministry of Cooperative Development in August 1987. An evaluation was undertaken in September 1990 to consider its reactivation. The purpose of the mission was to evaluate the effectiveness of CMPP as a tool for activating committee members and ordinary members to participate in the affairs of their societies and to make a recommendation on whether the programme should be reactivated or not.

Two questions were of particular interest: 1) why was the programme really suspended, and 2) what results can been seen of the programme given the dormant situation in which it finds itself? The evaluators spent considerable time looking into the first question and came up with several in-depth answers but they sought only impressionistic data on the latter. The following quotes from the consultants' report provide some information in formulating possible answers to the questions.

> The stopping of the project by the government seemed to have nothing to do with its value to the public. There seemed to have been a basic misunderstanding at a governmental consultative level between the Office of the President and the Ministry of Cooperative Development and the Kenya National Federation of Cooperatives, ICA, and SCC' (Alila and Obaso, p. 77).
>
> After instructions came from the Ministry of Cooperative Development that the CMPP programme be suspended, members of the public who had participated in it did not actually suspend the CMPP project in their cooperative development activities. This was mainly because the impetus they had picked was still honourable and relevant and easily complemented the well established cooperative effort and programmes in self-reliance (Alila and Obaso, p. iv).
>
> It is also significant that requests were made for CMPP during the reactivation indicating an interest in the programme despite the stoppage by the Ministry' (Alila and Obaso, p. 58).
>
> There is dominance and majority feeling from the field that the CMPP programme was good and needed to be continued. Several groups that were interviewed about the value of the programme in their activities were even surprised to learn from the consultants that the programme had been suspended. On the contrary, they were just wondering about what had caused delays in the programme's follow-up or continuation. As an idea, and in spirit, the CMPP was still very much on and in several cases factories and societies were ready to continue with it on their own with very minimal input from outside (Alila and Obaso, p. v).

Sustainability of local initiatives is a major issue in promoting participation. Many programmes report significant results while local efforts continue to be nurtured by outside animators, but what happens when such support is withdrawn? The hint of continued activity in the primary societies after CMPP was suspended is an extremely interesting point. Unfortunately, the dominating concern of the evaluation for discerning the institutional contradictions behind the suspension distracted from further investigation.

The consultants left no doubt in regards to their opinion about the future of CMPP in Kenya. The very first sentence in the body of the report reads: "It is recommended very strongly that the CMPP Programme be revived and continued" (Alila and Obaso, p. iii).

The consultants also put forward extensive suggestions about methodology. Once CMPP had been suspended, many suspicions and doubts about the ultimate purpose and motives of CMPP were raised. The consultants intensively examined the methodology while investigating these allegations. The resulting recommendations were, therefore, well considered within the political climate surrounding the question of CMPP reactivation and were subsequently incorporated into the implementation design described above.

CMPP in Tanzania

CMPP emerged in Tanzania as a part of development assistance to the Cooperative Union of Tanzania. CMPP was included as a substantial component of the "Regional Cooperative Support Programmes" (RCSP), funded by SCC, which were planned for the Morogoro, Central, and Coast Regions.

The concept of CMPP was first introduced in Tanzania when three facilitators from the ICA in Kenya travelled to Morogoro in March 1986 to conduct a demonstration CMPP seminar with the management committee and staff of the regional union. This initial exposure to CMPP was favourably received by the Morogoro union and led to SCC commissioning a two-week consultancy in November 1986 to consider possible ways that a pilot CMPP programme might be initiated in Morogoro. These subsequent recommendations of the consultancy were approved by CUT for CMPP inclusion into the RCSP.

CMPP in Tanzania became active when the Morogoro Regional Cooperative Union (MRCU) hired the first facilitator in February 1987. Two other full-time CMPP facilitators were hired by MRCU in April. The three new Morogoro facilitators spent three months working with CMPP in Kenya during April, May, and June where they completed an initial training programme in CMPP methodology. A week-long CMPP study tour to Kenya involving a dozen senior administrators from the MRCU and the ministry took place in May, providing union personnel with broader exposure to the programme. CMPP facilitators returned to Morogoro in June and began their work with primary societies in July 1987.

In July 1989, CMPP was expanded to Dodoma when three CMPP facilitators were hired by the Central Regional Cooperative Union (CRCU). Their initial training took place in Morogoro. CMPP was expanded once more with the hiring of three facilitators by the Coast Regional Cooperative Union (CORECU) in January 1990. They also received their initial training in Morogoro. In July 1989, the senior facilitator left MRCU and took up new duties at CUT as the "National Field Liaison Officer" and began working with all three regional programmes. A CMPP National Coordinator works with the programme on a part-time basis in Dar-es-Salaam, dividing his time with other CUT-related obligations. Ten full-time personnel are working with the CMPP in Tanzania: three each in the three regions and the one liaison officer based in Dar-es-Salaam.

The Implementation of CMPP in Tanzania

The village is the basic level of CMPP activities in Tanzania with the full "Cycle of Activities" taking place in villages. When the CMPP began in the Morogoro Region in 1987, most cooperative primary societies were composed of several villages. In these circumstances, complete two-day CMPP seminars are held in each village comprising a society. Self-help projects are planned in these seminars for implementation at the village level.

Once CMPP seminars have been held in every village, a society-wide seminar is held where representatives from each village come and report on the plans made during the village CMPP, including a review of the vision, obstacles, and proposals for the society as discussed in the villages. Some of the key questions in the society-wide CMPP seminar are these:

- what can this cooperative society do to provide services that would support the successful implementation of the village projects?

- what would this society need to do in order to better prepare itself for providing these services?

- what necessary changes might be required of this society if it is to provide high-quality services to its members?

These questions set the stage for planning society projects, which often involve considerable attention to the training of staff. The society CMPP seminar ends with scheduling society projects and naming coordinators just as is done in village seminars.

Since CMPP began in Tanzania, a national directive has come from the Cooperative Development Department (CDD) of the Ministry of Local Government, Community Development, Cooperatives and Marketing instructing each village to move toward registering its own separate co-op society. Some have argued that this policy creates a situation where many village-based societies will be economically unviable (Danida), which may well be true. However, the one village, one society policy has little effect on the operation of CMPP due to its focus on village-level activities. In fact, it simplifies it because it eliminates the need for holding seminars first within the villages and then for the entire primary society.

A few days prior to CMPP seminars, a special "Training and Education Meeting" (T&E) is held. Everyone living in the village is invited and CMPP hopes as many people as possible will attend. The purpose of the T&E meeting is to talk about the purpose of cooperatives and the rights and obligations of cooperative members. After making a general presentation to the entire population, a facilitator meets with women by themselves to discuss these issues in greater depth. During the T&E meeting, CMPP is also introduced to the whole village, clarifying immediately that CMPP will not be bringing any "capital inputs" under any condition. The list of representative participants who will attend the CMPP seminar a few days later is finalized in the T&E meeting.

CMPP in Tanzania intends to have approximately 40 people attend the seminar. People are invited by the three categories of men, women, and youth. It is explained in both the initial set-up meeting and T&E meeting that these participants should be truly representative of the entire village. This means geographic representation as well as economic. CMPP seeks a mix of sexes, ages, and economic well-being. It also means a mix of co-op members and non-members since everyone in the community is dependent upon the services provided by the cooperative.

Three workshops take place on the first day of the seminar: vision, obstacles, and proposals. All three workshops follow the same basic procedures. Teams meet by the divisions of men, women, and youth. Each team discusses the topic of the workshop and brainstorms items. In preparation for the plenary session, the teams select the five key points from their discussion which are then reported to the plenary. Items from each team are listed on the wall at the front of the room when team reports are given.

There is no attempt to organise any of this information into categories. Facilitators instead lead a reflective discussion after all of the reports have been given asking questions like:

- how are the lists from men, women, and youth similar? different?

- (men are asked) why do you think women said what they did?

- (women are asked) why do you think men said what they did?

- what values and concerns are revealed in these different reports?

- what questions of clarity would anyone like to ask another team?

These open questions from the facilitator release the group to ask each other questions on topics of particular concern. Discussions during the "obstacles" workshop especially become lively affairs as people tend to ask leaders a host of awkward questions on financial accountability. Rather than a systematic analysis of obstacles, the workshop becomes an informative discussion about troubling questions that may have been buried for a long time. The following "proposals" workshop then has participants consider practical solutions to these problems.

The obstacles workshop usually takes at least two hours to conduct, sometimes more if "hot" questions are being asked, while the vision and proposals workshops are normally completed within an hour and a half each.

The second day of the seminar begins with the "projects" workshop. Men, women, and youth are again divided into separate teams where they propose two self-help projects for the coming year. No external inputs are anticipated: the projects are to be accomplished through locally available resources. The issue of project ownership is discussed and a consensus reached. When projects are related to income generation, teams typically decide to form special "production groups" or "clubs" primarily composed of, but not limited to, the people involved in the teamwork. Reports are heard in the plenary and the facilitator leads a discussion about practical issues that must be resolved if the projects are to succeed. This workshop takes a couple of hours to complete.

Men, women, and youth return to the teams during the "implementation" workshop to plan detailed steps (how, when, where, and who) in organising work on the projects. These are reported back in the plenary session where each project is reviewed by other participants for anything that might have been forgotten in the implementation planning. The seminar then ends with a general discussion on coordination and potential problems that will need to be overcome once the projects have been launched. A wall-chart of the projects is presented to the village leadership for public display. The workshop is also usually completed in two hours.

Follow-up meetings are conducted by facilitators three months after the seminar. Besides reviewing progress and difficulties in project implementation, basic financial reports on all projects are given. Newly formed clubs also write a simple draft of by-laws. Facilitators guide this process by asking basic questions: "how is the membership of this club determined? who are the current members and how can new members join?

how will decisions be made? who needs to be present? who will speak for the club in public? how is money handled? who is responsible for accounting and where is the money kept? how will any surplus funds be distributed? how often does the club membership need to meet?"

CMPP in Tanzania is organised by focusing on groups of five societies within a district at any one time. The selection of societies is made through a dialogue with officials from the co-op union and the Ministry. The five societies should be located in two congruent divisions in a district so they will be relatively near to one another. Once a series of five CMPP seminars have been completed within a district, the "CMPP leaders seminar" is held. In addition to village and co-op chairman and secretaries attend along with relevant extension officers.

Tanzanian facilitators only conduct one follow-up meeting themselves. Part of the intention of the leaders seminar is to prepare local people to conduct "internal follow-up meetings," without the presence of facilitators, during the second and third quarters of the project year.

The Tanzanian "CMPP Cycle of Activities" for a cooperative is listed below. It identifies the minimal rhythm of contact a facilitator has with a society involved in the CMPP programme. As noted earlier, the Ministry's directive is rapidly eliminating the need for holding village and society CMPP seminars. This cycle is the basis of planning and budgeting for CMPP in Tanzania and will span little over one year to complete. Times will vary according to seasons of the year and geographical distances that must be travelled.

CMPP Cycle of Activities in Tanzania

month 1   confirm the five targeted societies in the district with union and government officials
            set-up visits to the societies and villages

month 2   training and education meeting in each village
            CMPP seminars with each village
            CMPP seminar with the society

month 3   monitoring visit to see progress of projects and to meet with leaders and coordinators

month 4   leaders seminar for village and society chairman and extension officers to discuss means of supporting MUWA project implementation

month 5   follow-up meeting with seminar participants

month 8 internal follow-up meetings without CMPP facilitators

month 9 monitoring visit to see progress of projects and to meet with leaders and coordinators

month 11 internal follow-up meetings without CMPP facilitators

month 14 final society CMPP seminar.

Each CMPP team in Tanzania is to have a chart posted on its office walls cross-checking this list of activities with every society and village where work is currently taking place. Each activity is marked and dated as they are accomplished. The tracking chart also serves as a tool for coordinating schedules across districts.

Results of CMPP in Tanzania

An assessment undertaken by the Popular Participation Programme, Department of Social Anthropology, University of Stockholm, provides a brief profile of CMPP work in Tanzania (Noppen and Fugelsang). Though the consultants were reserved in making any claims about long-term results, they did, however, note some short-term achievements:

- CMPP generally aroused enthusiasm as people obviously welcomed the opportunity to discuss problems and to communicate these to regional authorities, which were represented in the seminars by the union;

- CMPP provided a vehicle for channelling village energy into certain priority activities, usually infrastructure projects previously identified but for whatever reason had not yet been completed;

- modest successes were recorded for small income-generating projects, though the consultants questioned their long-term sustainability;

- some evidence suggested co-op membership did increase after the CMPP seminars, though the consultants suspected that mistaken expectations for access to a tractor may have been more of the cause for this than new awareness generated by the seminar;

several examples suggested increased "member awareness" following the seminars, one example being the withholding of tractor lease payments to the union because the union had failed to pay the levy to the society (Noppen and Fugelsang, pp. 47-48).

This assessment was instrumental in initiating several new alterations in the design and implementation of CMPP in Tanzania which are reflected in the description above.

Two major impact studies of CMPP were also undertaken by Sokoine University of Agriculture in Morogoro, Tanzania. These studies proved to be of limited value due to difficulties encountered with the methodology of the evaluation. Difficulties associated with using quantitative surveys in evaluating participation promotion programmes are examined later in Chapter 6.

CMPP in Zambia

CMPP in Zambia finds its institutional home at the Cooperative College. The staffing of the programme differs considerably from that of Tanzania and Kenya. In Zambia, there are no full-time Zambian personnel working with the CMPP. The National Coordinator is a Senior Lecturer at the College and divides her time between other teaching obligations. From July 1987 until December 1989, one Swedish technical assistant was assigned by SCC to work with CMPP on a full-time basis and served as the CMPP Co-liaison Officer during that time.

The initial introduction of CMPP to Zambia took place in November 1986 when an SCC staff member stationed in Zambia spent a month working with CMPP in Kenya. This led to the creation of a "CMPP Test Programme" for 1987. The Southern Provincial Cooperative Union designated four societies to be involved in the test. A CMPP study tour of senior cooperative officials from Zambia took place in Kenya during a week in April 1987. Prior to initiating CMPP activities in the primary societies, an extensive set of surveys were conducted to identify particular issues related to members' participation in Zambia. A special week-long workshop was held at the Cooperative College in June 1987 to alter CMPP methodology for an appropriate fit to Zambian conditions. This also provided a first training opportunity for future CMPP facilitators. The test programme began to conduct seminars in the four primary societies in July 1987.

CMPP was expanded to the Lusaka and Luapula Provinces in 1988. The facilitation of all CMPP activities in the primary societies is undertaken either by education extension officers from the provincial offices of the Department of Marketing and Cooperatives or by education officers from the provincial co-op unions. There are no full-time facilitators in Zambia. All of these officers, of course, have many other responsibilities besides CMPP. Due to the staffing changes that continue to occur, it is difficult to have a precise number of people who are actively working with CMPP as facilitators at any one time. Since CMPP in Zambia began its operation in July 1987, approximately 25 provincial facilitators have been trained and involved in programme implementation in one degree or another (Goransson and Saasa).

The Implementation of CMPP in Zambia

The primary cooperative society is the basic level of CMPP activities in Zambia. Thirty to 40 share-holding cooperative members are invited to attend the CMPP seminar. An invitation list is prepared by society officials following an initial set-up meeting by facilitators. Fifty per cent of those invited should be women.

Criteria for selecting societies for involvement in CMPP have changed over the years and have varied from province to province. Currently, the essential criterion is that societies chosen for CMPP should be restricted to those where the "Members Training Programme" (MTP) has been carried out prior to the CMPP seminar. MPP is a separate programme from CMPP and is conducted in many more societies than is CMPP. Its purpose is to educate village people about cooperative principles, co-op structures, and the rights and duties of cooperative membership. Though they are separate programmes, there is a direct connection between CMPP and MTP. The education officers employed by the provincial cooperative unions and the Department of Marketing and Education are the same people who both conduct MTP and facilitate CMPP.

Some provinces begin their CMPP seminars by having the participants who arrive early prepare a short drama about self-help. Drawing on their past experiences, these participants create a story about the successful overcoming of problems which typically cause projects to fail. When a quorum is finally formed and the seminar begins, this drama is performed by the group of people who have prepared it. This innovation in Zambia has been a unique one within the CMPP across the region. People thoroughly enjoy the presentation of these dramas and they undoubtedly establish a free and open environment encouraging people to contribute their ideas in the discussions. Unfortunately, some facilitators have complained that the dramas also miss their mark. Because they take place at the beginning of the seminar before the concept of self-help has been fully explored, misconceptions about self-help are often illustrated in performances. This has caused some provinces to eliminate the drama from the seminar agenda.

The actual work of the CMPP seminar in Zambia begins with the vision workshop which is followed in turn by the problems workshop. The first day of the two-day seminar ends with a brief discussion before the whole group on possible solutions to the problems. During the second day of the seminar, self-help projects are planned and an implementation schedule is created.

Men and women meet separately during the teamwork in all of the CMPP workshops. Teams report back to the group by displaying lists at the front of the room. This allows for a comparison of insights and makes sure that women's views are not lost. It is only during the last workshop of a CMPP seminar, at the point of implementation planning, that men and women meet together. The proposed projects from both men and women are integrated into a common calendar at that time. Four projects are planned, two by men and two by women. If by chance a project is planned by both men and women, the two are consolidated into one. The next twelve months is divided into four quarters and one project each is plotted into the three month blocks. Since every project is planned as a cooperative project, all aspects of the projects—coordination, procurement, income management—fall under the jurisdiction of the society.

Follow-up meetings are conducted every three months by CMPP facilitators following the basic design reviewing progress on the quarter's projects and discussing problems in implementation. The cooperative educational officers who serve as facilitators are often in the primary societies for activities unrelated to CMPP. During these visits on other business, they conduct "informal" monitoring visits by inquiring about project progress with society officials.

CMPP Cycle of Activities in Zambia

month 1   confirmation of targeted societies for CMPP
set-up meeting with society officials
CMPP seminar with the society
monitoring visits as occasion permits

month 4   first follow-up meeting

month 7   second follow-up meeting

month 10   third follow-up meeting

month 14   one year review meeting.

Since CMPP was initiated in Zambia in 1987, discussions have been held about the need for holding special events for "contact person training." The intention behind this idea is to bring together a few selected members from each society involved in the CMPP programme for a special training event. These members would then receive training in the management and sustenance of self-help projects. Initial implementation of "contact person training" has begun at the time of writing and no report of results is yet available.

Results of CMPP in Zambia

Two assessments of CMPP in Zambia have been conducted by external evaluators, one in September 1988 by Milimo and Uitto and another in May 1990 by Saasa and Goransson. The consultants of the second assessment used three principal criteria of measuring the success of the CMPP in Zambia: education and training; level of participation in the programme, particularly female members; and the level of success in the implementation of the projects planned in the CMPP seminars (Goransson and Saasa, p. 21).

In regard to **training**, the consultants found the Cooperative College possesses the needed institutional strength to continue to play an important role in CMPP. They applaud and encourage the decision to introduce the cooperative "members training programme" (MTP) as a complement to CMPP. The consultants found that society members are in serious need of more practical training on CMPP methodology.

The consultants found that though there was increased "awareness" about the need for a higher **level of women's participation**, the actual results of more participation by women in benefits or decisions was not substantial. They pointed out the false tendency to equate attendance with participation.

The level of **project implementation** by members was reported to be low by the consultants. They attributed this in part to the superficial thinking about project alternatives, anticipated costs and benefits, and project feasibility during the CMPP seminars. A detailed analysis of project implementation was made by the consultants in the Kabenda primary society in Luapula Province. This was then compared to the written reports submitted by CMPP facilitators describing the status of the same projects.

Several recommendations were made by the consultants concerning possible improvements in the implementation of the CMPP programme. In brief, the recommendations were:

- diversification of the CMPP network by way of consultations with other institutions for advice on feasibility and other assistance;

- continue the promotion of non-agriculture income-generating activities in CMPP, especially through the "liberalising" of lending policies of co-op organisations to support such projects;

- intensified training for people involved in CMPP at all levels, from advanced facilitator training to "Member Training Programme" and training for local CMPP coordinators;

- more time in CMPP (even if lengthening the seminar by a day) for members to consider project technicalities, including guidance from the facilitators on practical matters like applying for a loan

- seriously assess the reasons accounting for poor attendance at CMPP follow-up meetings

- continue follow-up activities beyond the current two-year design

- create guidelines in pamphlet form on how CMPP seminar participants can more effectively disseminate information to other members

- establishment of more concrete guidelines for inviting participants to the CMPP seminars

- projects requiring significant financial outlays should acquire professional advice on viability

- all primary societies should maintain autonomous accounts of deposits so they always know their current condition

- a study should be commissioned on the supporting institutional framework (policies, training, credit) for women's participation, especially in regard to income generation

- streamline the ZCF activities that may conflict with CMPP—gifts and grants should be carefully assessed vis-a-vis the possibility of compromising self-reliance;

- care should be taken that interest in women's participation does not inadvertently result in merely a greater burden for women to bear.

Many of these recommendations reflect the difficulties involved in translating a theoretical programme design into a living breathing reality. Zambia, more than the other national programmes, has had difficulty in establishing priority attention for CMPP. This may be due to the fact that Zambia, unlike the other countries, has never had full-time facilitators. On the other hand, CMPP in Zambia is much more fully integrated into the existing cooperative structures than in Kenya and Tanzania so that the long-term prospects for the programme might prove to be more promising than those in neighbouring countries.

Strategic Differences in CMPP Methodology

As the review above on CMPP methodology has demonstrated, subtle yet significant differences exist between the national CMPP programmes in Kenya, Tanzania, and Zambia. These reveal an interesting shift that is evolving in the national programmes and reflect differing strategic values. In one perspective CMPP is seen as a programme working through formal cooperative structures for the sake of **grassroots mobilisation**; the other aims at the **institutional strengthening** of existing cooperative structures through the enhancement of members participation. In each perspective a shadow of the other can be found, but the difference is fundamental and has huge implications for shaping future modifications of CMPP methodology.

The evolving nature of these two different aims can easily be seen in a comparison of national CMPPs, especially in the comparison of CMPP in Tanzania to that of CMPP in Kenya.

Grassroots Mobilisation

The phrase "grassroots mobilisation" is often suspect with many proponents of participation. Mobilisation, they argue, implies that content and objectives of development activities are determined by outside authorities before "target populations" become involved through more or less benign forms of manipulation. That is not the sense in which it is used here. Mobilisation refers to the breaking down of passive attitudes through nondirective and minimal intervention of facilitators and can be said to occur when people begin to see themselves as agents of their own development by initiating their own projects.

In Tanzania, the formal co-op structures serve as the "organisational infrastructure" for CMPP. Facilitators are employed by the cooperative unions and initial set-up activities for CMPP seminars are coordinated through cooperative extension officers and the primary societies. It works with and through the cooperative structures. But the emphasis of CMPP methodology in Tanzania is clearly geared towards mobilisation. Key aspects of its methods illustrate the fact:

- non-members, as well as members, are invited to attend seminars
- men, women, and youth plan their own separate projects
- ownership of projects is determined by group participants
- participants choose their own project coordinators
- project coordinators receive simple training in organisational skills
- follow-up meetings conducted by CMPP facilitators are held with all of the original seminar participants
- the formal cooperative society indirectly supports projects of newly formed "production groups" but does not control them.

These points maximize the involvement of people at a level below that of the official local leadership. It is a process that is very open-ended with participants making all important decisions every step of the way: what projects will best meet perceived needs, who should be involved, who will share in eventual benefits, who should play necessary coordinating roles, when should implementation activities take place, why are problems being encountered in trying to complete the projects, what can be done to overcome them? This does not foreclose the possibility that projects might be planned for the primary society as a whole. More often than not, however, new working groups are created who in turn control all dimensions of the projects undertaken.

The action-research of Verhagen in 1984 differentiated between informal "cooperation groups" and formally registered "cooperative organisations." In the same manner, newly formed groups resulting from CMPP intervention in Tanzania can be understood, in the context of official co-op registration, as "pre-cooperatives." Eventually, over time, as people become more confident of themselves and more perceptive about potential benefits which can accrue from collective action, they will hopefully begin to utilize the possibilities of cooperative structures. In contrast to top-down sponsorship, this is movement building of cooperatives from the bottom up.

The strategy of CMPP in Tanzania is, therefore, one of establishing a pattern of successfully managed self-help projects in order to create a fertile "participatory environment" for cooperatives where primary societies and a genuinely democratic movement can take root and grow.

Institutional Strengthening of Formal Cooperative Structures

CMPP in Kenya has moved in another direction. With recommendations from the October 1990 evaluation, CMPP is now prepared to operate with new methodological guidelines. These focus attention on strengthening the formal structures of cooperatives. One of the biggest concerns vigorously expressed by the evaluators was the fear that CMPP might create "parallel structures" to those of formally registered cooperative societies. Their recommendations clearly reflect this concern. Some key modifications found in the new guidelines are:

- only share-holding members of a primary society are to be invited to attend a CMPP seminar
- no special quorum is to be set for women's attendance in seminars
- suggestions for capital expenditure or income generation arising in CMPP seminars are to be forwarded to the society management committee who will then decide what, if any, official action will be taken

- only projects for minor infrastructure repair involving volunteer labour or production-improvement activities by farmers are to be coordinated locally
- only the officially elected management committee members representing the geographical area are to be appointed as project coordinators
- only the elected management committee members are to be invited to CMPP follow-up meetings, thereby excluding the original seminar participants (Alila and Obaso).

The new approach to CMPP in Kenya aims to enable cooperative leaders to become more sensitive and responsive to member concerns through the broadening of input into a planning exercise. In the process, members will hopefully become more aware of and interested in the society's activities. Potentially, this approach also creates a public forum of accountability whereby members can ask practical questions of the leadership. Involvement of members, however, primarily consists of contributing ideas about future directions, problems, and solutions which the elected leadership will then take under advice.

CMPP in Zambia sits somewhere between the programmes in Kenya and Tanzania. It certainly encourages all participants to attend follow-up meetings and project coordinators are not simply limited to the elected leadership. Given the nature of this discussion, however, the Zambian CMPP must be seen to give greater emphasis to institution building than grassroots mobilisation. Attendance to CMPP seminars is restricted to share-holding members; women meet separately from men during most of the seminar, but their projects are finally merged into a single calendar; all projects planned in the seminar are clearly under the direct control of the primary society; the large expanses of territory hinder any realistic possibility of many people working together in implementation activities. Accordingly, CMPP in Zambia basically seeks to expand members' input into planning and sensitize leadership to members' concerns.

Though the current design of CMPP in Tanzania has been presented as an example of grassroots mobilisation, this perspective is in constant danger of slipping away. In the regular self-evaluation meetings held by facilitators, proposals have continued to surface that, if incorporated into the design of the programme, would shift CMPP more toward an institution-building approach. Recent examples of these types of proposals are:

- government cooperative extension officers should be named as coordinators because they are in a better position to supervise and enforce implementation activities

- only members should be invited to CMPP seminars and all projects should therefore belong directly to the cooperative society.

And an even more radical proposal was once suggested:

- CMPP seminars would be much more effective if they could be conducted exclusively with the elected members of the management committee and thereby keep the confusing comments of members out of the planning altogether.

To date these have not been heeded in Tanzania, but they give an indication about the drift toward institutional strengthening and away from grassroots mobilisation.

Observations on Institutional Strengthening and Mobilisation

The obvious intent of CMPP's new design in Kenya is to reinforce and improve existing cooperative structures. It apparently places great faith in the democratic ideals that theoretically lie behind national legislation governing cooperative affairs. It also seeks to minimize risks. CMPP in Kenya opens up dialogue without fully releasing unpredictable forces that are difficult to control, whether they be a challenge to current leadership (through the "parallel structure" of locally selected project coordinators) or control of locally generated capital. Ultimately, the institution-building of CMPP in Kenya is an approach oriented more towards preserving the position of leaders than towards empowering the participation of ordinary farmers.

Significant benefits, however, for strengthening cooperatives can occur through participatory planning and they should not be slighted. The comparisons above are not intended to undermine the importance of trying to strengthen organisations. The persistent encounters with ineffective institutions across Africa should make that point self-evident. But the distinction between mobilisation and institution strengthening should not be simply ignored when discussing participation and cooperatives. Consideration needs to be given to both.

Of course, it must also be remembered that governments are not always hospitable to grassroots mobilisation. When people shed their passivity and become more self-confident, practical consequences are unpredictable. This often comes as an unwelcome complication, if not an outright threat, to many administrators. It is probably not a coincidence that CMPP in Kenya shifted its emphasis to organisational strengthening following the three-year suspension ordered by the Ministry of Cooperative Development. Other groups, too, have an interest in focusing on improvements within existing cooperatives. These vary from apex organisations to the donor agencies assisting them in their work.

The tension described in this section between grassroots mobilisation and institutional strengthening is not a new one and can be traced back to the very roots of CMPP when it emerged from the pilot work of The Institute of Cultural Affairs. On the one hand ICA was very involved in grassroots mobilisation with the "New Village Movement" (NVM). It also developed programmes specifically designed to strengthen organisations; this latter effort was through its work with LENS ("Leadership Effectiveness and New Strategies"). CMPP in Tanzania can easily be seen as an adaptation of the old NVM while CMPP in Kenya can be viewed as an adaptation of LENS.

A host of participatory strategies need to be prepared for use in the different situations. This chapter has explored a variety of approaches that have evolved within CMPP. Development workers must always accommodate themselves to the constraints and realities of operating in the real world. The issue for concerned pragmatists committed to participation promotion is choosing the most appropriate methodologies for the given situation and then making them work as effectively as possible.

Chapter 4

BABATI DISTRICT LAND MANAGEMENT PROGRAMME IN TANZANIA

The third field laboratory for testing MAP methodologies was found with the Babati "Land Management Programme" (LAMP). LAMP was initiated in 1988 with an agreement between the governments of Tanzania and Sweden and has since undergone several organisational revisions. Its basic aim throughout its history has been the improvement of land-husbandry practices across the district. Within the overall long-term objective of assisting sustainable and productive management and utilization of natural resources, the overriding strategy of the programme has been the promotion of self-reliance.

"The activities and projects in LAMP should be planned and implemented within the district by the people themselves and their organisations" (Swedforest, p. 5).

In this manner, LAMP has been designed to support project activities at all levels—district, village, and individual—rather than initiate new land-use projects on its own. The promotion of popular participation in environmental issues has thus been a major aspiration of the programme since its inception.

Its abiding interest and commitment to participation brought LAMP into contact with the MAP Project. With the SIDA office in Dar-es-Salaam acting as an intermediary, MAP was invited to assist LAMP in designing and implementing a two-phase participation approach in Babati: phase one was to be participation seminars with four pilot villages and phase two was to be district-level seminars with different interest groups. The intent of the seminars in the pilot villages was to demonstrate the potential for local initiative in land-management issues through grassroots planning. The intent of the district-level constituency seminars was to seek important input into the planning of district-wide projects that would be ultimately supported by the LAMP programme.

This chapter begins with a review of LAMP objectives and a brief description of MAP involvement with the programme. The second section highlights the first phase of MAP activities with LAMP: the collecting of base-line information and the conducting of participatory seminars in four pilot villages. The third section reports on MAP adaptations that were made for district planning seminars with five contending interest groups.

Objectives of LAMP

The LAMP programme in the Babati District is a programme designed to address the many environmental problems that exist in the area. These are numerous:

- decreasing agricultural productivity due to widespread soil erosion
- land abuse and uncoordinated land use by all sectors (agriculture, forestry, wildlife, livestock, and fisheries)
- inadequate water supply for domestic use caused by enviromental destruction and poor distribution systems.
- overgrazing caused by decreasing pastures arising from constant invasion of pasture areas by cultivators; encroachment of national parks and wildlife conservation areas depriving wildlife of natural migratory and reproduction areas
- destruction of water-catchment areas resulting in silting of dams, lakes, and rivers followed by subsequent floods

The LAMP programme aims to support the introduction of sound land-husbandry practices to secure sustained and increased production from the land and water resources of the district. As stated in its programme document, LAMP is

"convinced that such a development must be based upon the mobilization by the people themselves of their own resources. External resources can only support a 'process of learning by doing' and should not come in with ready-made solutions. By nature such an approach may lead to a slow start and call for a long-term perspective. The involvement from LAMP will be restricted to extra funding for village and district projects, and support to increase the capacity of the District Council to give technical advice and to serve the community. We have proposed a 'bottom-up approach," which means that the demand on funds and services in most cases will depend on requests from the villages on the basis of development projects initiated and planned by themselves. Programme progress will depend on the extent to which villages and villagers will respond to these new options for support and will come forward with viable proposals" (Swedforest, unnumbered).

LAMP thereby intends to work through the District Council. This is by the financial support of environmental projects and the delivery of various services to villages including environmental-related training. LAMP also intends to encourage the creation of a fund for environmental development, the "Mazingira Trust Fund" (MTF), to support village-level initiatives related to environmental issues.

The MAP Project worked with LAMP in two phases. The first phase involved the designing and conducting of **village planning seminars** in four pilot villages. The purpose of these participation seminars was for village people to identify priority projects that they could implement on a self-help basis. These seminars were not overtly focused on environmental problems. The intention was to allow environmental issues to emerge from the wider indicative concerns that are considered to be important by villagers. A follow-up analysis of the environmental implications derived from issues expressed in the village seminars was part of MAP's contribution to LAMP planning.

The second phase of MAP activities with LAMP involved the designing and conducting of **constituency seminars**. These events were to assist the LAMP office and the District Council in strategic planning for future work. This occurred through separate planning seminars for specific interest groups in the district. One seminar was for small-scale farmers; a second was for large scale farmers; a third for pastoralists; a fourth was for local non-governmental organisations; the fifth and final constituency seminar was for government administrators and elected officials. In contrast to the village seminars, the focus of these events was directly on the subject of good land management and sound environmental practices. The different views of the various constituencies helped determine priorities for LAMP project planning and implementation.

Participation Seminars in the Pilot Villages

MAP activities were implemented in four pilot villages selected by the LAMP: Endabeg, Managhat, Riroda and Himiti. The implementation procedures were divided up into four sequences for each village. These sequences were

a) set-up and preparation for each village
b) participatory base-line collection
c) two-day MAP seminar
d) documentation of each of these sequences.

The implementation was carried out by three LAMP project multipurpose extension officers in conjunction with the Tanzania national CMPP facilitator assisted by two officers from the MAP Research and Development Project office, Lusaka. The three LAMP multipurpose extension agents participated in all four sequences.

The implementation period was scheduled for one month, 1-31 August, 1989. This period included half a day to set up procedures in each village, one-day collection of base-line data together with the village community, two days seminar in each village and the necessary documentation. Specific questionnaires were designed for collecting base-line information from each village as were special procedures for the seminars.

The base-line questionnaire and the MAP seminars avoided a narrow focus exclusively on land-management issues. The discussions in the seminars were likewise unrestricted to environmental issues: the participants focused on the issues they themselves thought would be the most relevant. Thus, the base-line collection embraced a number of general socio-economic aspects of the village communities.

Formal follow-up meetings were scheduled to take place in each village approximately three months after the MAP seminar. In order to strengthen the mobilization and participation process, LAMP arranged for the multipurpose extension agents to work full time in the selected pilot villages to assist and encourage the village communities in their implementation efforts of the proposed projects.

The overall documentation of the implementation procedures and the analysis of base-line and seminar information was the task of the MAP Research and Development Project.

Base-line Methodology and Findings

The collection of base-line data was based on a participatory approach. Two main respondents were selected by the village community and some 20 representatives from different social categories of the respective communities were invited to participate in the base-line "dialogue" together with local extension officers. Women's participation in the dialogue proved to be more difficult than was originally anticipated and was severely limited due to the dominating presence of the male leadership.

The lengthy questionnaire was administered by two LAMP extension officers in conjunction with the national CMPP facilitator from CUT. The participatory approach in the base-line data collection served both as a means of involving a large number of villages and as a preparation for the MAF village seminars. The reliability of the data collected was in some cases questionable, particularly some quantitative aspects. The information was sufficient, however, to provide a village profile and a foundation for subsequent monitoring. The data collection was deliberately focused on general social and economic issues.

Despite economic and social differences between the pilot villages a number of common denominators could be found.

The **main crops** in the four pilot villages were maize, beans and pigeon peas. Coffee was mentioned as an important cash crop in only one village, Riroda. Several other crops were grown but sold on the alternative markets and information regarding the production and sale of these crops was not available. Considerable quantities of the main crops were also sold on the informal markets.

Farm inputs supplied to the villages were always in short supply with the exception of Riroda, the largest of the pilot villages. Only in Riroda did the quantity supplied and quantity demanded regarding seed, fertilizer and insecticide balance. Relatively few farmers seemed to be using "commercial" farm inputs. In Riroda, only 100 farmers used hybrid maize seed and only 50 used commercial fertilizers. Though many more farmers in the villages were using hybrid seed than were using commercial fertilizers, it was interesting to note that in discussions regarding the difficulties experienced by the cooperatives, the main supply of commercial inputs, the insufficient delivery of farm inputs was never brought up as a major constraint. The low number of users of commercial inputs, therefore, seemed not to be solely due to a low supply of inputs. Other factors were also involved. A clear relationship, for example, existed between the quantity of commercial inputs used and the availability of storage facilities. In the villages without a cooperative store, the use of inputs was considerably lower than in the other villages.

Concern about the local **cooperatives** was, however, similar among the villagers regardless of if a village had its own cooperative store or not. Lack of empty grain-bags, delayed payment for the produce sold to the cooperative and a delayed buying season were all major problems identified by villages. Only in one village, Managhat, did the participants of the study mention that the late delivery of fertilizers and seed caused a problem for the farmers. Two of the four pilot villages also experienced a shortage in basic tools, primarily hoes which had been ordered through the cooperative but not supplied to the farmers/members.

Livestock was an essential part of the prevailing farming system in all four pilot villages. The main economic and social value was focused on cattle but these were complemented by sheep, goats, donkeys, a few pigs and a relatively large number of poultry. The majority of households owned some cattle. With very few exceptions, livestock was comprised only of indigenous species. Altogether there were less than 30 grade dairy cattle, in the four pilot villages. Twenty-three of these are owned by households in the Managhat village.

All livestock appeared to be sold on the private/informal market. Very little "commercial" inputs were used in livestock keeping. Only one village had access to a dip; the other three villages had no access to services and drugs for their livestock. Only a few livestock owners seemed to use their cattle for transport or cultivation.

The availability of **local extension officers** was relatively high in all four of the pilot villages. Villagers all agreed that the extension services most needed were: agriculture, health and livestock, with some internal differences in the rating. This provided an interesting indication of perceived needs and priorities. Unfortunately, these mainly reflected the priorities of village males.

Few **training** opportunities seemed to have been offered to the villagers in the past for any of these three priority areas.

The current **farming systems** practices in the four pilot villages have created a number of constraints for the village communities. In random order, the following constraints were identified within the base-line data collection:

- lack of clean water for humans and livestock
- land shortage
- overgrazing and lack of adequate pastures
- lack of firewood and soil-conservation measures
- lack of basic implements as hoes and ploughs
- lack of improved farming and livestock practices
- lack of destocking measures and adequate supply of grade dairy cattle.

Village **infrastructural facilities** and projects in the four pilot villages all showed a conspicuous tendency to decay. Village tractors, milling machines, access roads and official buildings and village farms and village dispensaries were all classified as being in a relatively poor condition and were lacking essential spare parts.

The main reason for the limited success of current **village projects**, as identified by the base-line, was the lack of legitimacy and trust in village government and leadership. Funds for village projects had disappeared and village leaders provided no reports on profits, losses, nor general progress with village projects. The repeated pattern of poor participation in village communal projects was most likely due to 1) little popular support for projects planned by the village government, 2) over-reliance on external resources for project implementation, and 3) the fact that most projects had very limited relevance for the women.

Design of the MAP Seminars in the Pilot Villages

The village level seminars took place during two days, beginning at about 09:00 hours and concluding at about 15:00 hours.

The first day of a seminar was divided into three "workshops": vision, obstacles, and proposals. The vision workshop had participants consider the question "what development activities do you think need to happen in this village?" They were urged by the facilitators to be bold but also realistic in their thinking and to suggest activities that were actually possible instead of offering fantasies or wild dreams.

The vision question was intentionally broad and open-ended without reference to the issue of land management. Part of the intent of village-level seminars was to understand the perspective of villagers regarding their own aspirations and the problems that they feel to be frustrating them.

The next session of the first day, the "obstacles workshop," focused on the question "what has been preventing this village from accomplishing the activities described as the vision?" The third workshop, the "proposals," asked the question "what can be done by people in this village to eliminate or avoid the obstacles that are frustrating local development?"

On the second day of the seminars, participants discussed, selected, and planned self-help projects that they would accomplish without the benefit of out resources. Four projects were planned in each village, two suggested by men and two suggested by women. Each of the workshops followed procedures where individuals momentarily considered the focus question privately before moving into discussion teams. The women met together as one discussion team and the men as another. Within the discussion teams, individuals shared their ideas on the question. It was the responsibility of the facilitators to make sure that everyone expressed their ideas and that no one person dominated the conversation at the expense of others. After discussing all of the contributions, the team selected representative ideas to report back to the other team.

When the seminar reconvened as an entire group, team reports were given. The facilitators then led a discussion asking a series of questions:

How were the ideas of the men and women different?
Men, why do you think the women said what they did?
Women, why do you think the men said what they did?
What has been past experience with any of the ideas presented?
Which items seem to be central to the concerns of this village?
What resources are required to do these things?
How might we organise ourselves to obtain locally available resources?

Is some special income-producing activity needed in order for any of these projects to be completed?
If so, what income activities can be successfully undertaken?
How will this village go about doing it?
Who will manage the money?

The purpose of all these questions was to have the seminar participants think more deeply about their situation and the opportunities that were open to them through renewed organisation and planning.

The seminar ended by stating four self-help projects with beginning and ending times scheduled across the entire year. A wall-chart with visual images depicting the projects was prepared to display in the village office.

Comparison of the Village Seminars

Vision

Everyone of the four villages (and seven of the eight teams, indicating a shared priority for both men and women) mentioned **safe and clean water** as one of their primary concerns for the future. Each of the four villages (and again seven of the eight teams) also mentioned improvement and expansion of services at their local **clinic/dispensary** as matters of high importance for the future.

There was also remarkable consistency across the four villages in visionary declarations about the need for increased farm productivity. Every village mentioned **horticulture and nurseries** in their vision statements. Similarly, every village also voiced great concern about **improved techniques of modern farming and livestock keeping**. It is interesting to note that in every case, it was only the village men who listed modern farming and livestock keeping while the women exclusively named horticulture and nurseries. This largely reflects the division between sexual roles and responsibilities found in the villages. As those who are responsible for managing households and raising the family, women are interested in increasing subsistence produce and selling the surplus so making an income which they essentially control. The men, on the other hand, are very interested in the techniques of modern farming which enhance productivity of cash crops, the incomes from which they are most likely to control.

Road/bridge improvements was an item included in the vision discussions of three of the four villages. Himiti, the only village not to include such a statement, did have some other vision elements unique unto itself: "milling machine, child day care, and a village market."

The men in three of the villages mentioned the launching of **small industries** to be part of their vision; small industries include items like brick making, construction, and grain-milling. Endabeg was the only village not to mention small industries, while they were the only village to mention "cattle dip" and "go-down." Women in two villages included **local brew businesses**; women in two villages also placed **grade cattle** in their vision.

Obstacles

Formulation of obstacle statements during the seminar discussions did not produce the same degree of duplication across the four villages as was found in the vision workshops. A number of reasons might account for this. Whereas vision statements communicate simple and direct aspirations which are usually agreed upon quite quickly, obstacle discussions consider highly complex complications that have been frustrating activities for years. By definition, obstacles focus people's attention on difficulties, on what has been going wrong, on limitations and constraints. These are intricate matters which are inseparable from the very particular circumstances of any one specific village; reports on these discussions should be expected to reveal the uniqueness of each situation.

Yet similarities in the obstacles can be discerned from the four villages. Below, similarities are presented in five broad arenas. The obstacle statements which compose each category are identified by village and gender, e.g., an obstacle put forward by the women's team in Endabeg is marked (Ew) while one from the men's team in Riroda is (Rm).

Inadequate planning and reporting and unfulfilled accountability

- no meetings to discuss projects (Rw)
- no plan for health centre (Mw)
- no women's involvement (Rw)
- women not involved in village projects (Hw)
- no local brew plans (Mw)
- too many projects (Rw)
- no comprehensive plans though many projects Em)
- no plan for village market (Hw)
- village by-laws ignored in misuse of funds (Mw)
- mismanagement of the mill (Hm)
- growing demand on the dispensary (Rm)
- no maternity ward (Ew)

Unavailability of resources and prohibitive prices

- difficulties in obtaining grade cattle (Em)
- unavailable grade cattle (Mw)
- lack of bridges and culverts (Em)
- lack of experts in building bridges (Ew)
- bridges beyond local capacities (Mm)
- lack of mill spares (Hm)
- water equipment is expensive (Mw)
- high prices of building materials (Rm)
- high cost of road machinery (Rm)
- high prices and inflation (Hm)

Limited land and poor conservation

- springs are spoiled by cattle (Rm)
- livestock destroying existing water (Ew)
- lack of water (Em)
- unavailable pastures (Rw)
- deforestation (Ew)
- no land for nursery (Hw)
- small tree nursery (Rw)
- lack of land for farms (Rw)

Unavailable and unexploited training opportunities

- lack of knowledge in tree planting (Rm)
- lack of modern farming techniques (Rm)
- lack of knowledge in obtaining loans (Hm)
- lack of know-how to obtain loans (Mm)
- inadequate water survey (Em)
- no knowledge of how to make wells (Hm)

Poor coordination and working relationships with institutions outside of the village

- district doesn't see need for village clinic (Mm)
- government & party solicit too many contributions (Mm)
- no felt need for clinic outside of village (Hw)
- late arrival of agricultural inputs (Hm)

Proposals

The content of the proposals discussions often closely reflected the reverse of the obstacles named in the previous workshop. For example, men in Managhat said "lack of know-how in obtaining loans from banks" during the obstacles section and offered "villagers should be educated on how to obtain loans" in the proposals.

As a general trend, women tended to be much more practical in their proposals (e.g. "neighbouring villagers who use the clinic should contribute in building a toilet for the clinic," Rw) than the men were in theirs (e.g. "the government should regulate prices to fit the needs of farmers," Mm). Still, many serious discussions did take place in the proposals teamwork that point the way to future activities even though they did not result in the immediate planning of projects in the following section (e.g. "destock local cattle in order to switch to grade cattle," Rm; "make baked bricks for construction of the go-down," Em).

A major theme in the proposal discussions in all of the villages was a call for more thorough reporting and involvement of women in projects ("report on all projects," Mw; "all projects should be reported upon in open village meetings," Rw; "elect more women," Hw).

Self-help Projects

Only four types of self-help projects were finally planned in the seminars: collective farms, horticultural nurseries, small industries, and grade cattle.

The projects involving **collective farms** were all for the sake of generating income for some other desired project. Five of the eight teams in the four villages planned projects around collective farms. Two intended to use the resulting income for making improvements in their water systems, while the other three planned to use the money made from their farms for improving a clinic, starting a local-brew club, and re-establishing a milling machine.

Horticultural nurseries were planned in all four of the villages and by five of the eight teams.

Five of the eight teams in two villages planned for the initiation of **small industries** to earn income for other goals. Four of these projects were for the sake of improving water systems and one was for capitalising a local-brew club.

One team planned a project around expanding **grade cattle** within the village. It is interesting to note that though this project was planned by the men of Managhat, they had not mentioned the idea earlier in any of their discussions about the vision, obstacles, or proposals. However, grade cattle had been a major theme in all three of the earlier discussions by the women. It appears that perhaps the women were able to put forward their ideas to the men convincingly, once they had a forum for gaining the men's attention, hence the "cross-over" effect in planning the project.

Some Conclusions from the Base-line and Seminars

The base-line and seminars were primarily intent upon mobilising local activities according to village priorities. On the basis of these priorities, the MAP project extrapolated a number of observations and recommendations for the future design of LAMP activities in the district. In this manner, MAP played a **consultative role** with the LAMP programme in addition to its **mobilisation role** with the villages.

The recommendations from the MAP Project were made in the light of the fact that proposals made for the pilot villages in the original LAMP document and priorities expressed in the base-line seminars do not necessarily correspond. The recommendation made by the MAP Project, therefore, specifically addressed the issues that were thought to be necessary complements to the original project document. Below are the observations and recommendations made by the MAP Project in its report to the LAMP programme.

The report noted that any project design introduced by LAMP should be related to past and ongoing projects in the villages concerned. It is particularly important to discern why certain projects have failed in the past while others have succeeded in order to utilize this experience and to establish a frame of reference for villagers and project staff.

An important constraint within the pilot villages, and probably in other villages across the district as well, was the lack of legitimacy experienced by the **village government** and village leaders. Both men and women appeared to lack confidence in their village leadership. The MAP project counselled, therefore, not to work solely through the village governments on the assumption that they were the key ingredient for mobilising active local participation. The likelihood of project failure would be high, as previous project history in the pilot villages had indicated, if this strategy were to be repeated.

One important reason for the lack of legitimacy among village government was found to be the reoccurring demands for **contributions**, both physical and fiscal, from among the villagers. Villagers were unable to identify for themselves how they had personally benefited from these community projects. A combination of a high demand for contributions plus a low perception of personal benefits were a formula for low participation and project failure.

The government, parastatal and cooperative institutions which have a mandate to supply services and facilities to the rural areas, as reflected in the pilot villages, also experienced a **limited trust** and legitimacy. Rural markets function poorly, requests for inputs are not met and payments are not provided in time. In order to work through any of these institutions, it was obvious that a sense of trust and legitimacy had to be established if villagers were to seriously regard and appreciate future project proposals.

The discrepancy between identified needs and ambitions of the village communities and the facilities supplied was particularly obvious in the field of **training** of village individuals. It was symptomatic that the little formal training that has been provided in the villages did not correspond to the villagers' perception of relevant development needs. Such training appeared to have had little impact on successful planning and implementation of village projects.

Most if not all village projects showed a heavy bias towards male planned and conceived projects. Men identified the projects but expected the labour contributions to be provided by **women** (like the village farm) free of charge. The women were rarely committed to implement these projects since they had not been consulted. They were unable to voice their opinion as to whether the projects were relevant or not to the conditions of women. They have only rarely been provided with progress reports. Incomes generated by the projects were not channelled to women's groups or to individual women.

Suggested Guidelines from MAP for LAMP Project Design

The MAP Project made several recommendations on the basis of its work. First, it suggested that **the concept of target population be avoided**, i.e. providing services directly and exclusively for the four target pilot villages. Special attention tends to create external dependency and neutralizes the mobilisation process toward self-reliance. Instead, the MAP project recommended that LAMP should support the improvement of competent institutional services to all households and villages across the district on an equal basis.

One reason for previous project failures was the lack of integration of women in planning and redistribution of benefits from the projects. It was therefore necessary to develop project approaches which were **explicitly women-oriented**, obviously being appreciated and accepted by men.

The LAMP activities need to be focused on both individual and communal activities. However, MAP thought it necessary for attention to be given to the re-establishment of the **legitimacy of the village governments** in order to develop a foundation for future participatory work whether communal or individual. Attention would thus be focused on:

- Comprehensive schedule for follow-up meetings to the MAP seminars to create a forum for close contact between government and participants
- Seminars for village chairmen and leaders on accounting, progress reporting for both current development projects and those initiated by LAMP

- The inclusion of women in village leadership and the demand that women's active participation be a prerequisite for any facilities provided by the LAMP project
- A special format must be created for the MAP seminar follow-ups. Monitoring meetings must be focused on how the communities react to seminar planning and implementation (not only on the actual seminar participants) and how a project may be strengthened.

Previous or ongoing projects in the pilot villages provided limited benefit to those individuals providing actual project resources. It was therefore recommended that any LAMP assistance should enable villagers to consider the correlation between communal activity and personal benefits. Community-wide discussions should consider criteria for village communities' or individuals' needs before LAMP project resources were distributed. Such criteria might include:

- women's involvement and approval in planning procedures
- define necessary physical input from communities and individuals in order to become eligible for LAMP assistance
- level of necessary monetary input as criterion for receiving LAMP resources.
- sufficient administration of accounting capabilities to handle the resource input.

MAP suggested that an important task of the **multipurpose extension officer** might be to create and enforce criteria for possible recipients of LAMP resources. Whatever their ultimate tasks, a clear description of the expected activities of the multipurpose extension officers along with training for the work would be required if they were to be effective in carrying out their responsibilities.

There was a clearly conceived relationship in the villages between poor water, high livestock density, and current farming practices. It was also apparent that there was a male domination in water-project planning. Any water project and soil conservation measures must have a heavy emphasis on women's participation. Water project support by LAMP should not only require the implementation of new conservation practices but also financial contributions from the community as concrete criteria for readiness and interest in water development assistance.

A number of ongoing village projects were dormant or had failed because of **lack of spare parts and supplies**. These projects might be restructured on a sounder administrative basis; women's involvement in these activities would tend to make them more practical. The LAMP project might support this in terms of

- supply of spare parts
- supply of material for dispensaries, nurseries, etc
- supply of dip material, spares for milling machines, water resources
- supply of basic tools, hoes, ploughs, etc.

MAP recommended that a LAMP "material or spare-parts acquisition section" be formed to ensure the availability of necessary spares to repair broken machinery: this would not be a gift or a free service but a procuring service for which the villages or individuals would pay commercially justifiable prices.

There was a considerable need for improving the availability of **livestock and farm inputs** in the pilot villages. The availability of input would be an important task for LAMP. This should be complemented with **training** in those areas with a particular emphasis on those training needs identified by **women**. Possible training arenas might be: **health**, **horticulture**, **forestry** and **livestock**, all related to **soil conservation** and all of which were identified by the women as being important.

Both the base-line and the MAP seminars revealed a considerable village focus, particularly among the women, on the provision of **grade dairy cattle**. The procurement of grade dairy cattle may be one of the most important instruments in involving women in soil conservation. One possible approach to this issue would be for LAMP to provide grade dairy cattle at subsidized prices (probably one per household) to all those who apply and meet the criteria established, whether these applications originate from the pilot villages or not. A scheme might be designed where obtaining grade dairy cattle also required some destocking measures of local cattle. This procedure might be combined with direct purchases of dairy cattle or the exchange of local cattle for dairy cattle. Obviously, such a scheme of grade dairy cattle would need to be complemented with veterinary service, livestock training, planting of fodder grass and land conservation measures.

It was obvious that the MAP base-line studies and village seminars did not provide a comprehensive data bank for the four pilot villages or other village communities in the district. MAP recommended that special studies in particular areas would have to be commissioned in the future by the LAMP project. However, MAP urged that these studies should be presented and discussed not only with relevant district authorities but with representatives of the village communities as well and in such a way that they feel that these studies have a specific purpose and benefit for their own livelihood.

Constituency Seminars with Five Interest Groups

The second phase of MAP involvement with LAMP was the holding of "Constituency Participation Seminars" and took place in Babati in February and March 1991.

The intent of the district-level constituency seminars was to seek important input into the planning of district-wide projects that would be ultimately supported by the LAMP programme.

The constituency seminars were to be held with five different contending interest groups: 1) small-scale farmers, 2) large commercial farmers, 3) pastoralists, 4) non-governmental organisations, and 4) district administrators and elected officials.

The MAP project oversaw the conducting of seminars in the four pilot villages in August 1989 while the LAMP programme was still in the midst of its initiation period. The district-level constituency seminars were then scheduled to follow in April 1990. This scheduling was important so that constituency viewpoints could be included in establishing priority areas for the District Council as it prepared official proposals for submission to LAMP; the district proposals were due at the beginning of the new fiscal year in July 1990. The constituency seminars in April were postponed, however, when they coincided with the worst flooding to hit Babati in a generation.

The constituency seminars were delayed yet again when organisational disagreements between the Governments of Tanzania and Sweden threatened to undermine the entire future of the LAMP programme. These issues were finally resolved in late 1990 and the district constituency seminars were once again rescheduled to commence in February 1991, the time when they actually did occur.

In the meantime, operational pressure resulting from the various delays forced the District Council into submitting proposals to LAMP **prior** to the constituency seminars. The proposals submitted were prepared largely on the basis of information gained from the participation seminars in the four pilot villages. The allocation of LAMP funds for designated projects for 1991-1992 which will be channelled through the District Council totals MTAS 35.0 (one MTAS = US$ 5,000). The projects and budget amounts for 1991 - 1992 are as follows:

a) **Livestock**
   Grade cattle   3.7
   Livestock services   3.0

b) **Agriculture**
   Endabeg Valley (to include
   Sharimo, Endabeg, & Nakwa)   5.8

c) Land
     Land use programme in
     villages around Lake Babati   3.0

d) Community Development
     Administrative seminars in
     the villages   4.0

e) Natural Resources
     Forest establishment around
     Lake Babati   1.7
     Bee-keeping   2.0

f) Water
     Installation of water system
     in the Endabeg Valley   4.8

g) Savings for future projects   7.0

                 Total MTAS   35.0

The late negotiations also resulted in a significant shift in understanding about the proposed "Mazingira Trust Fund" (MTF). The fund was originally conceived to be an integral part of the LAMP programme (Swedeforest, page 16). It was, however, disallowed by the Tanzanian government. It was decided during the negotiations that if MTF was to become functional, it would need to be formed as a non-governmental organisation (NGO) with funding sources entirely independent of the LAMP budget. Subsequent discussions in Sweden revealed that the likelihood of finding such sources was very good.

By the time the constituency seminars were finally held, the original intent for them had been transformed. No longer were they held for the immediate purpose of shaping district priorities for LAMP projects. Instead they became educational events about LAMP and its activities and potential ways for solving the district's environmental problems, including an introduction to the possibilities of forming the Mazingira Trust Fund as an independent NGO. Though these topics might have a long-term effect on the planning of district conservation projects, the concept of the seminars enabling direct "input" by contending interest groups into LAMP's short-term planning process was lost.

Design of the Constituency Seminars

Two seminar designs were created to meet the different needs of the constituencies. The first four seminars with the NGOs, pastoralists, and the large and small-scale farmers all followed the same format. The seminar for the district administrators and elected officials was different from the others in that it summarised the proceedings of the previous groups and then focused on the question of successful implementation of LAMP which had projects already planned.

The initial seminars with the four groups took place during a two-day period. Each was divided into five working sessions which involved a mix of structured conversation and brainstorming in small sub-groups followed by reports and reflections with the entire group as a whole when it reconvened. All discussions were led by a team of five facilitators trained by the MAP project. The key points of discussion for each of the five sessions are described below.

Workshop 1: "Personal Hardships" Due to Environmental Problems

> Participants were asked to identify practical difficulties in farming or in their everyday lives that could ultimately be traced back to land management issues. These problems were considered in five categories: 1) land, 2) water, 3) natural resources (forests, etc), 4) agriculture, and 5) livestock.

Workshop 2: "Perpetuating Practices" that Cause the Environmental Problems

> In this session, participants were asked to consider the root causes that are underneath their experience of environmental problems, especially those that are caused by some form of human activity.

Workshop 3: "Practical Proposals" for Solving the Problems

> Practical proposals were made by participants concerning the practical actions that could be taken by people in their constituency to solve the problems named earlier. These were then prioritised by the group according to the five categories (land, water, natural resources, agriculture, and livestock).

Workshop 4: Reflections on "Proposal Implementation"

> Past experiences with each priority proposal were discussed by examining three key questions: 1) what have been the reasons for

past successes with this proposal? 2) what have been the causes of past failure? and 3) what can this particular constituency practically do to ensure the success of this proposal in the future?

Workshop 5: An Introduction to the "Mazingira Trust Fund"

The concept of the MTF as an independent NGO was introduced by staff of the LAMP programme. The presentation was followed by a lengthy period of questions and answers from participants about the MTF. Those who were interested in attending an organisational meeting for the MTF were asked to list their names and addresses so that they could receive timely notification.

The seminar for district administrators and elected officials took place after all four of the specific constituency seminars were completed. The last seminar reflects the responsibilities held by these participants for implementing the LAMP proposals decided upon by the District Council.

Workshop 1: Reports from the Four Previous Constituency Seminars

Sub-groups were assigned to look at the priority proposals that arose from each constituency. Participants were asked to choose the idea they considered to be the best from the constituency under their review, identify any confusing ideas that might have been made, add new ideas that might have been left out, and then recommend how the district might practically go about supporting the constituency's priority proposals.

Workshop 2: Review of District-wide LAMP Projects

The five major LAMP projects for the coming year as determined by the District Council were presented and initially discussed by the group. This discussion included the proposed budget for each project. Questions and answers enabled a thorough understanding to emerge in regard to the broad directions of the LAMP programme in the immediate future.

Workshop 3: Workshop on the Implementation of the LAMP Projects

Participants were asked to consider innovative means for implementing the LAMP projects. Rather than simply assigning each project to a particular department to implement on its own, possible cooperative ventures for an integrated approach were encouraged. In sub-groups, participants reviewed implementation steps, integration possibilities, major constraints, and the important "keys" to success.

Workshop 4: An Introduction to the "Mazingira Trust Fund"

The concept of the MTF as an independent NGO was introduced by staff of the LAMP programme. The presentation was followed by a lengthy period of questions and answers from the administrators and elected officials about the MTF. Discussion focused on the relationship of the proposed NGO nature of the MTF to the official structures of the government within the district.

Implementation of the Constituency Seminars

The four constituencies as determined by the District Council for these seminars were 1) small-scale farmers, 2) large commercial farmers, 3) pastoralists, and 4) non-governmental organisations. The fifth and final seminar was for administrators from the different governmental departments within the district and elected officials, i.e. members of the District Council.

In the preparation meetings for the seminars, the MAP Project had originally urged for the small-scale farmers to be divided into two separate seminars - one for men and one for women. Rural women are a crucial group intensely engaged in farming practices that have an immense impact on the environment. Yet their views are often slighted when men tend to monopolise discussions. The MAP project has experienced that the best way to highlight the insights of women is to provide a separate forum so that their views are not lost in the dominating talk of men. The idea of a special seminar for women was rejected, however, by the District Council.

The Babati District has four divisions with a total of 21 wards. Invitation letters were sent by the LAMP programme requesting each ward secretary to nominate one male farmer and one female farmer from the ward to attend the seminar. Emphasis was put upon the need for inviting a man and a woman; it was specifically stated that the temptation to send two male participants would be totally unacceptable. The small-scale farmers selected to attend the seminar were to be from among farmers who cultivated five acres or less. Forty small farmers equally divided between men and women attended the seminar on 19-20 February.

Pastoralists were also invited through the assistance of ward secretaries. Those invited included a mix of men and women. Though pastoralists by background and still in possession of large herds of cattle, the pastoralists who actually attended the seminar on 22-23 February tended to be those who had largely settled in one area or another into more or less permanent homes and farms.

The large commercial farms in the Babati District are all located in the one division where under twenty farms are currently in operation. All of these large farmers were invited to attend the seminar: only eight actually came on 26-27 February.

The NGO organisations invited to attend the seminar were either church-related organisations or groups associated with private development agencies. Invitations to this seminar were also sent specifically to some women's organisations. The invitation list was created by the local facilitators hired by the LAMP programme to work on the seminars. The NGO seminar was held on 1-2 March 1991.

The LAMP programme itself created the invitation list for the seminar for district administrators and elected officials. All of the important bureaucratic offices in the district were included along with a selected representation of elected officials. This seminar took place on 5-6 March 1991.

The venue for all of the seminars was the Babati Conference Centre and all were conducted in Kiswahili.

The MAP project worked with a group of five facilitators in conducting the constituency seminars. Four were from the Babati district while one came from outside. The outside facilitator was the national field liaison officer for the CMPP at the Cooperative Union of Tanzania in Dar-es-Salaam.

Practical preparations for the seminars began in earnest when this facilitation team of five participated in a two-week training seminar during November 1990 in Kibaha, Coast Region. Plans for the seminars were made at that time. In January, the Babati-based facilitators began carrying preparation duties by writing and delivering invitations on behalf of the LAMP programme. The team finally convened for immediate preparations and final training one week before the commencement of the seminars in February when Ms Omari and I arrived in Babati.

Report writing in Kiswahili took place in Babati by the facilitators after all of the seminars had been completed. A special evaluation session hosted by the MAP Project was held on 8 March at the Manyara Lodge. LAMP staff and all of the facilitators were in attendance at this final debriefing session.

Observations and Comments about the Constituency Seminars

Since the LAMP projects for 1991-1992 had already been decided upon before the holding of the constituency seminars, they became primarily educational events rather than participatory planning events for the shaping of short-term projects as had been originally anticipated. This undoubtedly took some of the urgency and practicality out of the seminar proceedings. Seminar participants entered into the discussions in a detached and relaxed manner realising that their comments would not have an immediate effect on the direction of LAMP.

Yet participants were clear that resolving environmental issues is of extreme importance to the long-term future of the district and they grappled with realistic ways of solving them. A number of major themes consistently ran across the seminars. There obviously exists, for example, a broad consensus for the need to introduce grade cattle while promoting a corresponding strategy for "destockiñg" herds of indigenous livestock.

Though the introduction of grade cattle will probably require a scheme drawing upon significant external resources, participants also identified a number of proposals that could be accomplished with a minimal amount of effort beyond local organising activities. Terracing, care for the environs of springs, and reforestation efforts through extensive planting of trees are three of the most common proposals discussed. The seminars thus served as a serious starting point for considering such locally oriented projects. The seminars should be viewed as a beginning rather than as an end in the search for firm conclusions.

Discussions on topics like these thoroughly prepared participants for the subsequent discussions on the Mazingira Trust Fund. People in all of the constituencies were extremely interested in the prospects of the MFT. Through such an organisational vehicle they began to see the real possibilities of obtaining modest funds to support local environmental initiatives. Their enthusiasm for the MTF was enhanced by the prospect of it being operated as an non-governmental organisation. This idea was both novel and exciting for them. Over and over again throughout the seminars participants voiced their scepticism about the District Council's ability to effectively manage and supervise major projects. People looked forward to the prospects of creating a new democratic organisation that might be held more directly accountable for its activities. If the seminars are any indication, the MTF should enjoy widespread support by people living in the rural areas.

Participants in the seminar for the administrators and elected officials were only mildly interested in the ideas that emerged from the preceding seminars. Their foremost attention was given to discussions about the implementation of the LAMP projects which had just been approved by the District Council.

The seminar facilitators attempted to have district officials consider innovative means for implementing these projects. Two important words in preparing participants for these discussions were "integration" and "collaboration." An example was given in regard to the grade cattle project. Rather than having the district office of the Department of Agriculture and Livestock organising every small detail in areas where they have little or no experience - arranging logistics for obtaining and transporting grade cattle, administering loans to farmers for purchasing grade cattle, making collections for repayment, etc. why not "collaborate" with an experienced NGO like the Heifer Project International to oversee the implementation of the project.

Innovative collaboration of this sort was a difficult concept for most of the participants to grasp. They largely considered "integration" to be a matter of working across different ministries. Conventional approaches were the norm. The proposal from community development is an example. Instead of designing a new programme to support emerging local initiatives aimed at environmental issues (like many of the proposals just described in the four constituency seminars), the idea put forward by district officials was to train villagers in the vague "role and responsibilities" of village government. This proposal may well be based more on the existence of an educational programme found in the files of the community development office than on the manifest needs of mobilising rural people to solve environmental problems.

The reflective questions asked by the facilitators after reports on these conventional ideas did slowly begin to have an effect: imaginations were awakened and thoughts began to move toward more innovative approaches. As in the four preceding constituency seminars, the seminar for administrators and elected officials was an educational event that started a dynamic thinking process; no firm conclusions were reached. The seminar seeded the imagination of the officials in attendance, but further nurture by the LAMP office is most assuredly necessary if true innovation is to take root and grow.

The discussion on the Mazingira Trust Fund by district officials revealed the difficulties faced by the LAMP office. Whereas participants in the constituency seminars were excited by the prospects of the MTF being independent of government control, the district officials took a different stance. The content of some proposals being advanced by very senior officials for the MTF was extremely alarming, chief among them being a strong recommendation to build new secondary schools within the district. This, of course, has nothing to do with the intended purpose of the MTF to support local environmental development projects.

But as with all of the discussions in the seminars, conversation was being initiated, not ended. The seminars widened the scope of dialogue about the evolving environmental crisis in Babati and the intentions and prospects of the LAMP programme. The seminars increased the numbers of people actively involved in dialogue. Perhaps even more importantly they attracted viewpoints from different types of people not often used to having their thoughts and opinions solicited for serious consideration. The constituency seminars enabled the LAMP programme to take a few more steps in a long journey toward establishing a participatory approach to addressing environmental problems that ultimately can only be solved by people themselves.

Chapter 5

IRDP IN ZAMBIA'S EASTERN PROVINCE

The "Integrated Rural Development Programme" in the Eastern Province of Zambia (IRDP/EZ) has provided another field laboratory for the testing of MAP methodologies. The origins of the current IRDP/EP are found in the Intensive Development Zone (IDZ) which was introduced in 1972 as part of bilateral assistance between the Zambian and Swedish governments. In 1979 the name was changed to IRDP/EP to reflect the wider inclusion of more communities across the province. A third phase was introduced in 1986 when services were extended to rural communities in the context of decentralisation through District Councils. The IRDP/EP is now scheduled to come to an end in 1993 and is actively engaged in a "phasing out" programme between now and then.

MAP began its relationship with IRDP/EP in October 1989 when initial discussions took place about future collaboration. This set the stage for a series of "Branch Development Seminars" that eventually took place in the Chama District. The MAP Project was then involved in subsequent follow-up activities with the Chama work including an extensive evaluation in June 1991. Beyond the work in Chama, MAP has assisted IRDP/EP in creating a programme design for a series of seminars to form local "Project Maintenance Committees."

Branch Development Seminars in Chama

The "Branch Development Seminars" held in the Chama District were particularly interesting because they combined community-wide planning with the training of local leaders in practical skills of organising and implementing self-help activities. Personnel of the Institute of Cultural Affairs in Zambia were contracted by the IRDP/EP to assist in carrying out the programme.

Branch seminars in Chama were conducted by teams of three or four facilitators composed of ICA staff, district council employees, and extension officers from the Social Department of the Ministry of Labour, Social Development, and Culture based in the district. The seminars were conducted between May 1990 and December 1990. Seminars were conducted in 54 of the 69 branches during that time.

Design of the Branch Development Seminars

Each seminar is a five-day event with three major sections: 1) the Branch Development Planning Meeting (BDM) held on the first day of the seminar; 2) the Community Leadership Training Programme (CLTP) held on the second, third, and fourth days; and 3) the Work-day Demonstration (WD) held on the fifth and final day of the seminar. A brief description of the content and activities of a "branch development seminar" follows.

The invitation to attend the BDM is open to all members of the branch. An attempt is made to have as many women as men attend. After introductory remarks on the first day of the seminar, the participants discuss their **past achievements, present community development projects,** and **future hopes** for the branch. This discussion is recorded on the "vision work-sheet chart" in the participants' workbook with lists for the past achievements, present projects, and future hopes and dreams.

The session is then shifted to the identification and discussion of **constraints.** Analysis of constraints is done in small teams of 8-10 participants. A list of constraints is then recorded on the "constraints work-sheet" after the small groups reconvene.

The next session identifies **proposals** that will enable the branch to overcome the constraints discussed earlier in the session. The proposals are then translated into practical **self-help projects** which are grouped according to the "five areas of human activity," i.e. economic, political, social-cultural, science-technology, and defence-security. There is no limitation on the number of projects that may be identified from the list of practical proposals.

Projects are then prioritised and a **two-year implementation calendar** is made. The first year of the two-year time-line is divided into quarters while the second year is divided into six-month periods. The participants then set the targets for the projects scheduled to occur in the first quarter and list steps and tasks needed to implement the projects. Facilitators have participants create a one-month time-line. This schedule shows when work is to be done in the next four weeks, identifies who will carry out tasks, and how the work will be accomplished. In planning the one-monthly timetable, people also assign project supervisors and schedule specific work-days.

Selection of participants for the Community Leadership Training Programme is then made as the BDM ends with a session reflecting on the day's activities, lessons, and experiences.

The CLTP begins on the second day with a short discussion of development trends to establish a historical perspective to social and economic change. Activities then centre around discussions and lessons on how to "Do Our Own Projects" (DOOP). After a general introduction, the participants are divided into small teams according to the geographical sections of the branch in which they live. The small teams discuss projects that could be implemented at the section level. The objective of the small teamwork is to have participants learn skills related to the planning and implementation of self-help projects. During the workshop, people practice forming a project task force and discuss how they can organise themselves for effective project implementation.

Small teams are selected to create and perform dramatised role-plays on the implementation of projects planned during the BDM, e g. clearing pathways, digging toilets and water-wells, formation of a task-force, or organising a work-day, etc. After a lunch break, the sections continue to meet in small teams before presenting their work to the whole group for analysis, comments, and adjustments. The DOOP process concludes in a "Branch Assembly" where the section plans are reviewed in the context of the whole branch.

The third day of the seminar is devoted to lectures and workshops on **leadership style and effective communications**. Participants examine and discuss various styles of leadership and the different effect these styles have on people who participate in planning meetings or work on community projects. Similar discussions occur on issues of effective communication within the branch. Participants then create role-play dramas to demonstrate good and poor aspects of communication practices and leadership styles. Additional work is then done on how to make a comprehensive calendar of activities which takes into account all community activities and the agricultural seasons.

The fourth day of the seminar includes a lecture on **development principles**. The focus of this presentation is on economic, social, and human (cultural) principles and how they apply to local situations.

Another important lesson of this day is on **project material** preparations. A discussion on different sources of outside assistance for larger long-term community development projects then precedes a lecture on **project proposal writing**. After this, the participants are divided into small groups of four to practice writing a proposal to an external donor or the district council concerning a project identified in the BDM. Each small group presents a report to the whole group for reflections, comments, and adjustments.

The fourth day ends with a lesson on **preparing community work-days** followed by participants actually specifying work to be accomplished on the next day for one of the projects planned during the BDM. They designate tasks, assign supervisors, arrange for materials, and notify workers who have anticipated a work-day since the BDM was held earlier in the week.

The fifth day of the seminar is the **"Demonstration Work-day"** which involves all participants of the BDM and CLTP. Facilitators work alongside the participants in completing the day task. At the end of the seminar each of the CLTP participants take their participants' workbook with them for future reference.

After the branch training seminars have been conducted, the **"Monitoring Circuit Follow-up"** (MCF) is the next important step in providing continuity. The IRDP/EP has since funded the first round of MCFs in Chama. At the time of this study, MCFs have occurred in five out of the six branches covered by the study.

The MCF is a two-day event which has been carried out by two facilitators, one from the ICA and the other from the district council. During the first day the facilitators visit different leaders at their homes. During the visit they discuss and record progress on projects and set-up meetings for the next day. The second day starts with a community meeting in which reports covering the previous three-month time tables are reviewed. The afternoon of the second day is then devoted to the DOOP review and the second leaders' meeting. A new three-month timetable is an important output of the MCF.

"Ward Planning Events" (WPE) are a recent addition to the series of seminars that have taken place in the branches. These two-day events were designed in January 1991 after the completion of the BDMs and CLTPs across the district. In the ward events, representatives from the branch seminars come together to share reports on the plans they made in their BDM and subsequent progress on the branch's self-help projects. Following this reporting session, a workshop is held to determine priority projects for the ward as a whole which will be submitted to the district for possible inclusion in the District Development Plan. On the second day of the WPE, a plan is made for the continuing work of the ward development committee. If no committee exists, then one is formed during the WPE including the election of officers.[a]

The WPE is the final event in the series of seminars, though follow-up meetings may continue to occur in the branches for an indefinite period of time.

Results from the Branch Development Seminars

The IRDP/EP commissioned an evaluation study of the Chama seminars in June 1991 (Chapeshamano and Bergdall). The study sought to determine what, if any, increases had occurred in the areas of local self-help activities, branch meetings, communication of information, women's involvement in decision-making, local income-generation, and training activities. The study also evaluated effects of the branch seminars within the district council. The findings of the consultants are summarised below.

A significant **increase in self-help activities** was found to have occurred in the branches in the twelve-month period after the seminars when compared to the twelve months that preceded them. The type of activities varied but mostly involved the construction of needed infrastructure like schools, wells, storage sheds, etc. Formation of new organisational groups such as women's and youth clubs also increased. The projects that were actually implemented in the branches were not necessarily those stipulated in the three-month or one-year BDM calendars since continual review of priorities in the branches resulted in several changes.

The seminar played a major catalytic role in establishing a clear sense of **branch identity** among the people. Most people suggested that this shift in focus from the ward to the branch was because of knowledge gained during the seminars.

The number of local residents actively involved in branch development efforts also increased. This was largely due to the growth of self-help activities. Similarly, an increase in the number of meetings held in the branches was seen to have occurred. Most of these were informal branch development meetings and special group meetings (e.g. clubs) rather than official meetings called by ward and branch chairmen.

There was **no substantial increase in income-generation** in the branches. The most important source of income for the branches consists of donations by the branch members, i.e. an informal tax for specific project requirements. The donations were not a standard fee nor were they collected regularly but were made as particular needs arose. Special groups like clubs, in contrast to the branches, did realise modest increases in their income-generating projects after the branch seminars.

Women's involvement in decision-making was found to have increased following the branch seminars and was carefully documented in the consultant's report. This involvement in decision-making was enhanced primarily by women's increased attendance at branch meetings. The growth in the formation of women's clubs was another factor contributing to women's ability to influence decisions.

Communication between branches and the district council remained at a constant level after the seminars due to the rigidly defined and formalised channels of communication. Communication within and among branch members appeared to improve in relation to increased meetings and branch development activities. In some branches new channels of communication based on new branch activities, such as schools, were used since the branch seminars took place.

The seminars had little impact on the planning and realisation of **training in practical skills.** There was little training actually taking place in any of the branches although a new demand for home economics courses for women was discernable.

District officials believed that, as a result of the seminars, it was possible to create a responsive District Plan based on the "bottom-up" approach with substantial proposals from branches and wards. This was in sharp contrast to the previous practice of setting development priorities for the district in governmental offices. This change in official attitude towards planning for development is attributed to the branch seminars. District officials also expected an increase in demand for materials and financial assistance from the branches as the latter increased their self-help development activities.

The district council had no financial or material resources to respond favourably and support branch self-help development efforts. The poor income base in the council excluded any major support to branches beyond a modest programme of follow-up and monitoring. It was, however, within the technical capacity of the council to continue providing staff to the branches. The council also held access to ministry staff who could provide technical advice and guidance.

One particular recommendation from the consultants' report merits comment. IRDP/EP obviously hoped that the seminars would help to instill a sense of self-reliance within the branches and encourage new income-generation. Though many new self-help projects were accomplished, villagers often held the view that such successes were a step toward showing potential donors that they were "worthy" of external support for other projects. In fact, many branches had already written and submitted proposals as a direct result of the CLTP's lesson on "proposal writing".

Income-generation, on the other hand, was found to be almost nil. Yet this should not come as a surprise since no session in the CLTP focused on the issue. The consultants recommended that in the future the Branch Development Seminars would benefit from dropping the session on "proposal writing" and substituting a new session on forming "income projects". This is particularly important in the light of the district council's admitted inability to provide material assistance to the branches for self-help projects and the general trend toward fewer donors, rather than more, operating in Chama District.

Project Maintenance Committees

For 20 years IRDP/EP has worked with local communities in funding a number of projects. These have varied from the digging of water-wells to the construction of school buildings. Many of these IRDP projects have since deteriorated because of poor maintenance. As the phasing-out document prepared by the IRDP/EP clearly states, realistic aims and objectives have to be taken into account for optimizing project impact during the remaining time of the programme's life. "The foundation of the IRDP/EP phasing-out policy is based on two main objectives for the current programme: 1) to increase the incomes of the rural poor and 2) to increase social and political awareness in rural areas" (IRDP/EP, p. 6).

In order to achieve these two objectives "it is necessary that IRDP/EP focuses its project work on **sustainability and maintenance**. It is unlikely that IRDP/EP would be able to create a sustainable institution of the current District Council structures. Therefore, IRDP/EP should aim at creating sustainable individual projects on a local level through supporting local institutions and local communities, to rehabilitate and maintain already existing facilities which have been assisted and/or financed through IRDP/EP" (IRDP/EP, p. 7).

As a part of its winding-up activities in the next two years, IRDP/EP wants to compile a final inventory on the status of these projects and establish local maintenance committees to sustain the projects in the future. To accomplish these aims, IRDP/EP designed a programme for conducting two-day "project maintenance committee planning seminars" which utilise an adaptation of MAP methods.

A maintenance seminar is composed of four sessions: 1) a review of the "current situation" of the village IRDP project, 2) identification of major maintenance tasks, 3) creation of a maintenance implementation plan, and 4) organising a project maintenance committee. As many people as possible living in the community are invited to attend the seminar.

The first session, the review of the current situation, begins with an introductory discussion about the project: when was it begun, how many people benefit from its presence, what hardships would be caused if it were to no longer continue? This is followed by a physical inspection of the project. When participants return from the visit, the IRDP/EP facilitator has the entire group complete a prepared "inventory" questionnaire that describes the current condition of the project. This session takes about two hours to complete.

The second session, identification of major maintenance tasks, begins by dividing the entire group into small teams. Each team is no larger than 15 people, so the number of teams depends upon the total number of participants in attendance. Men and women are sent to separate teams where a brainstorm

list is created of all of the maintenance problems/tasks that can be remembered
from the physical inspection of the project. These team-lists are written on
large sheets of paper or index cards for presentation in the plenary. After all
teams have reported to the group, duplicate tasks are put together and the
composite list of tasks is prioritised. This session is completed in about two
and a half hours. It ends the first day of the seminar.

Session three, creating a maintenance implementation plan, occurs on the
following morning. The group is divided into two large teams that include
a mix of men and women. Each team is assigned to consider one of the two
priority tasks as identified on the previous day. In the teams, implementation
plans are created for the task using a work-sheet that asks questions about
materials, tools, required labour, and scheduling. The teams reconvene in a
plenary session to hear reports.

After hearing the reports and discussing questions from the participants,
the group is again divided into teams, this time separating men and women.
The teams discuss the following questions:

- What has been the past experience in doing maintenance tasks in
  this community? Give some examples of past successes and past
  failures
- Why were you able to succeed when you did?
- What caused the failures?
- What can you do now to overcome these problems?
- Consider the two maintenance tasks just planned. What activities
  planned are traditionally those of women? of men?
- Will these traditional roles cause a problem in successfully
  completing the maintenance task? (facilitators will need to push
  for insights based on their own experience of potential problems)
- How might these problems be overcome?

A reporter from each team summarises the discussions and reports to the
group in a plenary. After the reports have been heard, the facilitator ends the
session with a question to the group: "based on these discussions, what will
be the keys to REALLY succeeding with these maintenance tasks?" Session
three takes about three hours to complete.

The fourth and final session of the seminar organises a maintenance
committee. The group is not divided into teams; the whole session takes
place with the entire group of participants. The facilitator leads discussions
by asking a series of questions: what are the responsibilities of the
"Maintenance Committee?" how does the committee need to function? who
should collect and hold the money? how can you ensure that money is not
misused? After the criteria for choosing committee members is discussed,
nominations are made and a maintenance committee is elected. The session

ends by scheduling the next meeting time. Session four lasts approximately four hours. With its conclusion, the seminar is brought to a close.

District officers make periodic monitoring visits after the seminar to the newly formed project maintenance committees as a part of their other on-going work in the rural areas.

At the time of writing, these seminars have just begun to take place across the province. No results are, therefore, yet available. The description of the programme design does, however, provide one more example of the flexible applications that can spring from MAP methodology.

Chapter 6

MONITORING AND EVALUATING THE IMPACT OF MAP

A major objective of the MAP Project was to develop new techniques for monitoring and evaluating the promotion of participation. This chapter reports on MAP experiences in this regard. It begins with a review of problems encountered in various evaluation studies of CMPP. The second section describes the methodology devised by the MAP Project for its own research with monitoring and evaluation. The following two sections report on monitoring activities with two villages in Babati after the conducting of MAP planning seminars. The final section of the chapter offers some interpretations of the Babati monitoring exercise.

Difficulties in Evaluating Participation

Evaluating participation programmes poses many problems. Several were identified during the "Workshop on Popular Participation Approaches and Democratization of Rural Development Projects in Zambia" co-sponsored by the MAP Project and the Institute for African Studies in November 1989. A primary problem, the delegates suggested, is that participation has often been regarded as a "means" for achieving development objectives rather than as a particular "end" in itself. Participation is thereby subjected to criteria and measures that are far more appropriate for traditional "project" evaluation than the evaluation of an on-going "process."

Projects have specific objectives and anticipated outcomes that are essentially fixed. A process is open-ended and evolves according to unique conditions and events that occur within a group or a community.

Monitoring and evaluation exercises are commissioned for a variety of reasons. They can assist in project planning and fine-tuning of implementation practices. They can assess impact or offer an analysis of cost and benefits. They can supply data when important decisions must be made; evaluations are especially in demand when the future funding of a programme is in question. Formal evaluations are thus often used as justifications for big decisions. The seemingly scientific objectivity of cold numbers is reassuring in such situations and may explain much of the preference for quantitative methods over qualitative ones in project evaluation.

An inclination for quantitative methods especially places the evaluation of participation in a precarious situation. In evaluating a process rather than a project, it is crucial to examine developments that are by their nature unpredictable. This is a task best accomplished with qualitative methods.

Outcomes of participation promotion are far too open-ended for forecasting specific anticipated results. Because of countless factors involved, anything except the most general of variables is difficult to predict. Many of the qualities associated with participation, e.g. "increased awareness" and "growing self-confidence," are in themselves intangible and require indicators unique to each situation. Numbers alone are of limited value in evaluating such indicators. Attendance at meetings, for example, can easily be counted but that is not the same as "participating" in meetings.

Description and interpretation are much more valuable for drawing conclusions about participation than judgements based on measurements. Inductive thinking takes precedence over deductive thinking. As one authority has pointed out, evaluation using qualitative analysis "is guided not by hypotheses but by questions, issues, and a search for patterns" (Patton, p. 15).

Problems in Evaluating CMPP in Tanzania

The Department of Agriculture Education and Extension, Sokoine University of Agriculture in Morogoro undertook two extensive monitoring exercises in regard to CMPP. The purpose of this work was to determine the impact of CMPP on the social and economic activities of the primary societies and in the villages.

The monitoring work of Sokoine University was the only evaluation activity in the three national CMPPs to utilise a purely quantitative approach. Two different monitoring exercises were undertaken, one in October 1988 and a second in July and August 1990. The same three consultants were involved in both monitoring exercises. All were in the Department of Agriculture Education and Extension at Sokoine University. Though there was some compatibility in the two exercises which allowed for some limited comparison over time, these were essentially two different exercises.

The sampling process of the first monitoring report was done at three levels: co-op society, village, and households. The **society sample** consisted of ten societies divided into two groups. The five experimental societies were the ones involved in the pilot programme of CMPP. Five control societies were selected in neighbouring areas and were not involved in the CMPP. The questionnaire used in the society sample had ten key variables: co-op membership, villages within the service area of the society, numbers of employees, equipment owned by the society, number of members having credit, money in the bank, turnover, crops procured, village projects, and society projects.

The **village sample** consisted of 40 villages and was also divided into two groups. All 25 villages located within the service area of the five CMPP societies were included in the experimental group. Fifteen villages from the five control societies were selected, three each from the five societies. Key variables for the villages included village projects implemented in the period of 1987 and 1988; proposed projects that were not implemented; constraints with project implementation; equipment and condition; and distance of each village from society headquarters.

The **household sample** consisted of one hundred households. In each of the 25 villages, data was collected from four households. Two of the households' respondents were men and two were women; out of these two one was a cooperative member and one was a not a cooperative member. The household questionnaire included variables on sex of respondents, co-op membership, marital status, access to cooperative services, satisfaction with cooperative services, CMPP participation, food security, and individual participation in projects. Figure 3 illustrates the data-collection design for the first monitoring report.

Figure 3. Design for Data Collection in First Monitoring Exercise		
	experimental group	**control group**
Society sample of 10	original 5 societies involved in the pilot CMPP	5 neighbouring societies not involved in CMPP
Village sample of 40	all 25 villages composing the 5 CMPP societies	15 villages: 3 each selected from the non-CMPP societies
Household sample of 100	4 in each of 25 villages: 1 male member 1 male non-member 1 female member 1 female non-member	none

The second monitoring report collected information for two samples, one for societies and one for villages and did not focus any attention on households. The total sample of societies was 15. Data was collected from ten experimental societies--the original five of the pilot programme plus five new societies involved in the second phase of the programme--and the five original control societies. Thirty villages composed the village sample, two villages each from the areas of the society sample. Figure 4 illustrates the design from the second report.

Figure 4. Data Collection Design of the Second Monitoring Report		
	experimental group	**control group**
Society sample of 15	10 societies involved in CMPP activities: the 5 original pilot societies and 5 new societies	the 5 original societies from the first monitoring report
Village sample of 30	20 villages: 10 from the pilot societies and 10 from new CMPP societies	10 villages: 2 each from the 5 control societies

"Out of the survey of all societies and their respective villages, the following information was gathered for the second monitoring report:

- population composition of villages
- number and composition of society members in the society villages
- assets of societies and villages
- number and qualifications of society employees
- training of society employees
- existence and quality of records and documents
- services available to society and village members from society
- input supply, types, timeliness, distribution, loan repayment, and problems affecting both societies and villages
- crops procurement: types, timeliness, storage facilities, payment, and other problems
- major crops grown for cash and food
- society and village projects - types, number, participation, extent of implementation and general problems related to these projects
- CMPP projects: types, number, participation, extent of implementation, and problems" (Rutachokozibwa et al., p. 2).

These variables and the data-collection designs indicate the high ambitions that were held for these studies at their outset. The intention was obviously to make a careful scientific inquiry into the broad social and economic impact of CMPP. These high ambitions, however, proved to be very elusive when data from the evaluation exercises were finally analyzed.

The evaluators had a very difficult task in drawing conclusions about participation on the basis of answers to questionnaires with predetermined variables. One of the evaluators concluded in a later document that "the methodology used in the two monitoring studies suffered from at least the following:

- it used mostly invalid indicators of success
- it did not focus on the process, no attempt was made to evaluate the extent of participation
- it was unrealistic to expect that after only two years there would be significant differences in the selected variables between CMPP and control villages, particularly since all cooperative societies are suffering from serious problems, most of which cannot be solved by CMPP and which, therefore, limit the potential of CMPP
- it used structured interviews which were carried out only once (for one or two hours) per respondent which obviously failed to capture a lot of useful details
- further details were lost in the aggregation of the data by using statistical analysis, whereas more descriptive and interpretive presentations of the data (in the form of short case studies) would have been more appropriate" (Mattee, p. 6).

The CMPP evaluations in Tanzania demonstrated the need for a more qualitative approach to evaluating participation.

Problems with Evaluating CMPP in Zambia

The success with which members implement self-help projects planned during CMPP seminars is often used as an indicator for measuring CMPP results. All of the CMPP evaluations employed this approach in one degree or another. Some of the conclusions reached through these measures illustrate the problems involved in effectively evaluating participation.

The 1988 assessment in Zambia examined the implementation of projects in all four of the societies involved in the original CMPP test programme. Each society had planned four self-help projects during their respective CMPP seminar. Below are the results they found.

"The Kasiya MPCS in Choma District seems to have performed the best among the four societies. During the first planning seminar, the society had identified the following projects for the community:

(1) to start operating the hammer mill
(2) to train board members in cooperative leadership
(3) to repair all the eight depot slabs
(4) to form a women's club

In the course of the year, the society was able to start operating the hammer mill, train all board members and to repair five out of the eight depot slabs. Only one project was not implemented, namely the formation of the women's club."

The two other societies, Choongo and Chitanta, were able to make progress on at least two of the self-help projects that they planned during their CMPP seminars. Of the four societies, the evaluators dropped Sinazeze to the bottom of the list in their comparison of successful implementation of planned projects.

"At Sinazeze, only one project was implemented. At the beginning of the year, the society had proposed:

(1) to acquire training in improved methods for growing cotton and maize
(2) to buy two bicycles
(3) to start a women's club
(4) to buy a hammer mill

The society only managed to buy a hammer mill during the one year time-line. In this way, Kasiya rates highest in achievement while Chikanta and Sinazeze rates lowest" (Milimo and Uitto, unnumbered).

The consultants had to labour under many practical constraints, as they explained in their report, including severe time limitations for accomplishing their field work. Time constraints most likely account for the simple presentation of achievements found in the report. Their manner of rating achievements, however, leaves many important questions unanswered when considering the impact of CMPP.

What was involved in the Sinazeze purchase of the hammer mill? What resources did they use to buy it? From where did the resources come? How did members in the society organise themselves? What problems did they have to overcome? In most Zambian villages, the purchase of a hammer mill is an extremely big accomplishment if done entirely through local effort. One can well imagine that if the society itself raised all of the resources for the purchase, then a priority of that magnitude would cause them not to have time to focus attention on other projects. Completing one major project at the expense of inaction on three others would be understandable. Of course, if a charitable organisation came in from the outside and gave them a 100% soft loan to buy a hammer mill, then the significance of the purchase would be viewed in a very different light altogether.

Discerning the role played by CMPP also raises many questions. For how long had the society been planning to buy a hammer mill? Was it a new idea raised for the first time in the seminar? If it was an old idea, how had CMPP effected the society's efforts to complete the purchase? How successful had the society been in implementing projects prior to the CMPP seminar? Did it already have a pattern for accomplishing ambitious plans like buying a hammer mill or had it been plagued by failures?

The answers to all of these questions appear to be crucial in understanding the impact of CMPP activities. The purchase of the hammer mill in Sinazeze, even though it was the only project completed, may have been a far more significant accomplishment than the completion of three out of four projects in a another society. Or maybe not. Only through careful investigation into the process of implementation, which goes well beyond a basic rating of completed projects, can an answer be provided. As the case of Sinazeze demonstrates, concluding interpretations depend upon a complex web of circumstances; simple statistical comparisons lose sight of these subtle distinctions.

Methodology of Evaluation as Conducted by the MAP Project

The difficulties and problems experienced in the external evaluations of CMPP described above led the MAP R&D Project to experiment in evaluating participation. The evaluation techniques that were eventually formulated drew upon recent publications related to participation and evaluation and monitoring.

Observations on Evaluating Participation

Peter Oakley is one of the most prolific writers working today on the subject of participation in rural development. He has written extensively on both theory and practice. Among his work is a book on evaluating social development programmes in general and a field manual for monitoring and evaluating FAO's "Peoples' Participation Programme" in particular.

Oakley advocates a combination of qualitative and quantitative methods for evaluating participation. Due to the "process" nature of participation as opposed to a "project" nature with predetermined objectives, qualitative methods are indispensable for interpreting the results of participation programmes. The successful evaluation of participation requires the holistic approach found in the use of qualitative methods.

The purpose of qualitative methods is to "avoid creating an evaluation monster of isolated, unrelated and out of context parts" (Patton, p.18). Participation promotion projects are complicated matters and evaluating them are particularly difficult enterprises. "The task is to provide a comprehensive understanding of the complex reality, or realities, surrounding the project: in short, to 'illuminate.' In his report, the evaluator aims to sharpen discussion, disentangle complexities, isolate the significant from the trivial, and raise the level of sophistication of debate" (Parlett and Hamilton, p. 99).

Oakley suggests that evaluating participation is best conducted when an evaluator has several occasions to monitor activities over an extended period of time. This, of course, is expensive, but a "snap-shot" approach of collecting information at a single moment severely limits an evaluator's understanding of the evolutionary process of participation. Regular and continuing contact is needed when participation is understood to be a dynamic process rather than a static project.

He also argues that evaluation of participation requires a high degree of familiarity between the evaluator and the subjects of the evaluation. Such familiarity is usually shunned in traditional evaluations because of the perceived need to preserve objectivity. This, however, negates the possibility of observing subtle changes. "Qualitative evaluation demands participation and commitment of the evaluator and discourages detachment and distance, characteristics of other approaches to evaluation" (Oakley 1990, p.5).

Oakley makes another relevant observation: evaluating participation should not be considered synonymous with the concept of "participatory evaluation." The latter may well be included in the former, indeed it would be a gross contradiction not to include it given the general bottom-up nature of participation promotion, but participatory evaluation cannot be a substitute for evaluation per se. "The evaluation of participation is the evaluation of a discrete process, whilst participatory evaluation is a form or technique of evaluation which is relevant in evaluation exercises across the sectors in rural development" (Oakley 1990, p. 19).

These observations about evaluating participation programmes were drawn upon as the MAP R&D Project designed its own approach to evaluating the impact of participatory planning seminars in two Tanzanian villages.

Evaluation Methodology in the Babati District of Tanzania

As described in Chapter 4, the MAP project assisted the Babati Land Management Project to conduct participation seminars in four pilot villages in August 1989. Two of these villages, Managhat and Endabeg, were selected arbitrarily to serve as case studies before activities commenced in any of the four villages. The monitoring and evaluation exercise began in August 1989 and was completed in August 1991.

Base-line data was collected through the completion of a prepared questionnaire The questionnaire was initially completed one week before the planning seminars took place. The very same questionnaire was then used again to collect information during the following two years. This data was collected in both villages during August 1989, August 1990, and August 1991.

Thorough notes were kept on the seminar proceedings. Every comment made by a participant during the plenary sessions of the planning seminars was recorded. The seminar occurred on two days and followed the basic format of MAP seminars: vision, obstacles, proposals, self-help projects, and implementation plans.

In August 1990, one full year after the planning seminars had taken place, **participatory evaluation meetings** were held in both of the villages. These meetings were attended by the same participants who had attended the original seminars. They evaluated their progress on projects planned the year before and created new plans for the coming year.

Between the annual August events (base-line data, seminar, and participatory evaluation meetings), **monitoring visits** were made to each village in March 1990 and March 1991. Information was collected during these visits through extensive interviews with seminar participants and with key informants from the villages and district. Over 100 interviews were ultimately conducted.

All of the evaluation activities described above took place on five different occasions spanning a 24-month period and were conducted by the same two individuals: the MAP Project Specialist (and author of this report) and an extension officer from the district office of the Ministry of Agricultural and Livestock Development. This allowed for the development of a thorough familiarity with the participatory process as it evolved in the two villages.

Managhat Village Case Study

The village of Managhat is located ten kilometres south of Babati town on the road to Dodoma. The population grew from 1,536 in August 1989 at the beginning of the evaluation to 1,649 in August 1991. Most of this increase was due to new births rather than the arrival of new immigrants. Managhat has grown considerably in the 1970s and early 1980s with the arrival of families from Arusha and Moshi. These immigrants were largely from the Meru and Chagga tribes. Today about half of the village population is composed of people from the native Irawk tribe and half from the new immigrants of the past 10 to 15 years.

Farming is the primary economic activity, the major crops being maize, beans, pigeon peas, and coffee. Most families keep some local livestock, though six families maintained a total of 23 grade cattle in 1989 and 1990. Five of the families owning grade cattle were among the new immigrant arrivals of the past 15 years while only one was of the native Irawk. The co-op membership in 1989 was 301 and grew to 310 by 1991.

Facilities owned by the village government include a tractor and a maize-milling machine. Two privately owned tractors are also found in the village. All three tractors are available to farmers on a rental basis. In 1990, the village tractor was hired by 79 different farmers while records were not available concerning the hiring of the privately owned tractors. Two privately owned ox-carts were in the village in 1989; this number grew to five by 1991. A constant total of 20 donkeys were privately owned by eight families.

Discussions and Plans from the MAP Seminar in Managhat

The seminar was originally scheduled to take place on the 18th and 19th of August 1991. On the 18th, however, only three women were in attendance so the seminar was postponed. The seminar began on the following day when the women's quota was reached. A total of 26 men and 16 women attended.

Men and women largely agreed on their **vision** for the future of the village. Problems of water were a big concern. People had to walk too far to collect it and the village springs were increasingly being spoiled by the watering of too many cattle. Villagers were also concerned about access to health care. Three priorities subsequently emerged from the discussions: **clean water, a local dispensary, and modern livestock keeping**, e.g. reducing large herds of unproductive traditional cattle through a transition to smaller numbers of high-grade dairy cows.

Though these three were clearly the big priorities, the men also indicated a need for road repair and a desire for launching some small industrial activities like carpentry. The women suggested they would like to see the village establish a tree and vegetable nursery and a village owned local brew club. They said a local-brew club was important so that men would stay at home rather "than go wandering endlessly in a search for brew elsewhere." They also thought that a local-brew club would help to keep money within the community.

Participants met in teams of men and women to discuss **obstacles** to realising the vision ideas. The women said they had many questions about these projects and selected a spokeswoman to ask questions on their behalf when they returned to the plenary session. In the plenary, reports were made from the men and women's teams.

After the team reports, the discussion on obstacles was dominated by questions on the status of the village water project. The women were angry because they were poorly informed about development activities in the village. Nothing had been reported on the water project. They had heard informally that the village government had received a donation of water-pipes and wanted to know if this was true.

The village leadership tried many evasive answers saying that the village now had two newly dug water-wells. Yes, the women said, they understood that, but what about the water-pipes? The leadership then said that water-pipes had been received but that since no one in the village had the technical expertise to lay them the village government was now waiting for government extension officers to come and assist. The women asked if the pipes were properly stored and if so, where. Finally, the village chairman came forward and confessed that the pipes had been stolen shortly after their arrival. This led to further discussion on the need to locate and punish the guilty and how to ensure that such theft would not be repeated in the future.

Information was also shared on the status of the desired dispensary. The chairman informed participants that government policy stipulated that only one dispensary should be built within a ward and that a neighbouring village had already been selected for their area. This led to further discussion on why this information had not been shared before.

The discussion was obviously a difficult one for the village leaders as they were forced to account for their actions. At one point a woman asked why the village government always acted in secret. This set the stage for the **proposals** workshop when a number of different suggestions were made on ways people could be kept informed about the activities of the village government.

On the following day, a number of **self-help projects** were planned. The women planned to start a one-acre nursery for trees, fruits, and vegetables. They also hoped to start a "local brew club" and reactivate the eight-acre farm belonging to the UWT club, i.e. **Umoja wa Wanawake wa Tanzania** (The National Women's Organisation of Tanzania). The men identified two projects: reactivation of the water project and modern livestock keeping within the village.

Developmental Process Following the Managhat Seminar

Modern livestock keeping

Information collected in the base-line questionnaire prior to the seminar established that six families in Managhat owned a total of 23 grade cattle. A former district chairman of the **Chama Cha Mapanduzi** (CCM), the ruling party of Tanzania's one-party state, was the only Irawk farmer in Managhat who at the time of the seminar kept grade cattle; he owned six. He reported that for many years he had received a lot of requests for the use of his bull but that these requests were always made by people who lived outside Managhat. People in Managhat, he said, preferred their large herds of traditional cattle.

He was surprised, therefore, when immediately after the seminar in August 1989 he was suddenly besieged by Managhat villagers with questions about grade cattle. Many asked about using his bull. Two Irawk women even came to ask if he would trade one of his grade cows for two or three of their traditional cattle. This, of course, was impossible because grade cattle are worth much more than local cattle but it indicated a dramatic new interest among Managhat residents about high-quality cows. When he asked why they were now interested in grade cattle after all of these years, he was told about the seminar and discussions for keeping modern livestock.

The man selected to be the coordinator for the livestock project was a member of the village council. He confirmed that immediately after the seminar many people were interested in finding ways of up-grading their herds. He himself visited the Ministry of Livestock and Agriculture to discuss ways that they might assist people in Managhat with their project. An extension officer suggested cross-breeding through artificial insemination as one possibility, but the project coordinator learned that it would be quite sometime before the Ministry was prepared to assist in that way. Resources were not yet available.

Investigations of this type continued for several months without much concrete result. They were, however, very useful in introducing people to the detailed requirements and special difficulties involved in the keeping of grade cows. People learned, for example, that grade cows were best cared for on a "zero grazing" basis, i.e. when fodder is brought to the cow rather than releasing the cow to graze at will. This led many farmers to plant special grass in anticipation of eventual cross-breeding with help from the Ministry.

Then in March 1990 a completely unexpected opportunity arrived in Managhat when the village was approached by "Heifer Project International" (HPI) about participating in a grade cattle scheme.

HPI is an international non-governmental organisation that provides grade cows to small-scale farmers through a systematic programme of training and preparation. HPI works through existing local organisations, e.g. churches or village governments, etc., with an offer to donate ten cows to individual farmers via a mutually agreed upon selection process managed by the organisation. After attending some basic training in the proper care of grade cattle, farmers prepare for receiving a cow by planting one acre of special feed grass and building a shed. When these tasks have been successfully completed, HPI gives one cow to each of the ten designated farmers. In turn, these farmers are obligated to donate the first female calf born from their cow back to their local organisation who then passes it on to another farmer in the group.

After the HPI official introduced the programme, 28 farmers in Managhat attended the training sessions and immediately began to prepare for receiving cows. The village government council, who was asked by HPI to act as the local coordinating organisation, decided that the ten farmers who most successfully met HPI's preparation requirements would receive the first ten cows.

HPI had previously donated cows to three other villages in the Babati District: Himiti, Bonga, and Hraa. Another neighbouring village, Singe, was approached by HPI at the same time as Managhat. Singe selected 20 farmers to prepare for receiving HPI cows.

During the 12 to 18-month preparation period, HPI staff regularly visit farmers to monitor progress on the planting of pasture grass and building of sheds. The HPI representative during this time commented on the big difference he found between Managhat and Singe. Managhat meetings were well attended and preparations were on schedule while meetings in Singe were poorly attended and preparations were slow or non-existent. Though the expressed interest in grade cattle was the same in both villages, Managhat was better motivated and organised in its efforts. The HPI representative was pleased to see Managhat farmers helping one another in their planting and construction.

The MAP Project made its final monitoring visit to Managhat in August 1991. Three weeks earlier in July HPI had finally delivered its first shipment of five grade cattle to Managhat and Singe. Four of these went to farmers in Managhat and only one went to a farmer in Singe. People in Managhat were excitedly awaiting the arrival of another 15 cows whereas they had been anticipating only an additional six! Because only one farmer had successfully completed the required preparations in Singe while over 20 had done so in Managhat, HPI decided that those cows designated for Singe would be redirected to Managhat instead as soon as HPI obtained them. This was expected in the very near future. HPI's national director in Arusha confirmed this shift to Managhat to be true.

Reactivation of the water project

The water project had taken off with some false starts a couple of years before. A church organisation in Arusha donated pipes. Trenches were dug through village-organised communal labour only to learn later that they were dug in the wrong place. This mistake had been learned after the fact through consultations with the district water engineer. Then as was revealed in the planning seminar in August 1989, the pipes had been stolen and the project came to a standstill.

Plans were made during the seminar to commit income from the 60-acre village farm toward expenses related to the water project. Furthermore, participants suggested that the village council consider collecting 200 shilling from every able bodied resident in the village to provide additional capital for water development (one US dollar = Tsh.150 in August 1989).

On the day after the seminar, the facilitation team encountered the village chairman on the road to Babati: he had just made the ten-kilometre walk into town to confer again with the district engineer about seeking his assistance in reactivating the Managhat water project. The chairman was pleased that the engineer had promised to come to Managhat and draw plans for the proper placement of trenches for future water-pipes.

Later in the year a completed set of drawings was presented to the village government in January 1990. The water project was subsequently discussed in meetings of the village government. The costs of purchasing pipes and taps, however, were much more than they had expected and only Tsh. 2,700 had thus far been collected from the villagers. The biggest disappointment concerned income from the 60-acre village farm: all money from sale of the produce had gone to repair the village tractor after a major breakdown. Discussions with district officials raised the possibility of obtaining a donation from the "Community Development Trust Fund of Tanzania" (CDTF).

At Managhat's participatory evaluation meeting, 15-16 August 1990, the village decided to submit a proposal to CDTF. The coordination team acted immediately after the seminar and met with district officials to help them prepare the CDTF forms on the very next day, 17 August. In total, they requested assistance for Tsh.240,000.

In April 1991 the Managhat village council was informed by CDTF that they would be unable to assist them in 1991 since they had decided to fund a similar water project in a neighbouring village. But CDTF also informed them that Managhat would be the most likely recipient in the district to obtain a 1992 CDTF grant.

Nursery for vegetables

The women decided in the August 1989 seminar that they wanted to create a horticultural nursery. Though they hoped to see trees and fruit in the nursery, vegetables were the primary concern. Women wanted to have access to additional vegetables so they could improve the nutritional value of their meals. Besides making seedlings available, women saw the project as an opportunity to learn about basic horticultural practices so they could individually establish small nurseries of their own in future.

The women participants in the seminar wanted the nursery project to be independent of the local UWT club and were very vocal in stating their case. This proposal was favourably received by officials of the village government and they promised to designate some appropriate public land for establishing the new nursery.

A UWT club has long existed in Managhat village. Though it has eight acres of public land designated for its use, no crop had been planted since 1986. It was in that year that UWT activities began to decline because of a failed consumer shop. Women in the village had donated money to the shop but it vanished and was never accounted for. Thereafter, most village women lost confidence in the UWT leadership and the club largely became inactive.

The women met to organise work on the new independent nursery and to follow up on promises from the village government shortly after the seminar. The village government provided an area and further assisted the women in February 1990 by assigning the village tractor to plough one acre of land. Afterwards, 30 women participated in a work-day to smooth the ground and plant tomatoes. Shortly after these were planted, Babati was unfortunately struck with the biggest floods of a generation and the seedlings were all destroyed.

By the time the women were able to get their households back into working order after the disruption of the floods, the ground at the nursery had become too hard for hand cultivation. The village tractor was also out of service. The women organised a work-day with borrowed oxen, but the ground proved to be too hard for this as well. Further activity for the nursery was then postponed for the following year.

Plans were for made for re-initiating the nursery during the participatory evaluation meeting in August 1990. Shortly thereafter another meeting was called and over 30 women attended. An idea was introduced that perhaps some money should be collected from the women to buy pesticides and fertilizers for the nursery. This had disastrous results for the nursery because it reopened old wounds related to the disappearance of money from the consumer shop three years earlier. Old accusations were once again raised and many of the women left the meeting quite upset.

When a subsequent work-day was called to plant the nursery again only half a dozen women appeared. They were too few and the project was again abandoned for the time being. Bitter incriminations about the old consumer shop continued to be the topic of gossip among village women.

The village government finally took action in January 1991 and called for the election of new UWT officers. These were the first elections since before the failure of the infamous consumer shop. A meeting was called and the old UWT leadership were all conspicuous by their absence. The women who did attend elected a new local UWT chairperson.

In contrast to a popularly elected chairperson, the local UWT secretary is a special party position and follows a different electoral procedure. The village chairman, who is also the local head of the party, himself made the nomination for the new secretary and submitted the name to the UWT district office for final approval. The district office confirmed the name and the woman was then notified that she had been officially elected. The new secretary was the same woman who had served as one of the coordinators for the nursery project.

In April 1991, five women were selected among 15 Managhat residents to attend a month-long programme at the "Training for Rural Development Centre" (TRDC) in Monduli. Both of the coordinators for the nursery project attended. After they completed the agricultural training in Monduli and returned home, they promptly restarted the nursery as an independent project separate from the UWT. By August 1991, a quarter acre was successfully planted with Chinese cabbage. Though a few other women joined in the planting, the bulk of the work was done by the women who had gone to Monduli.

Once the cabbages had been planted and were ready for harvesting, many other women came and asked to join the group. They were told, however, that they would need to wait for the following year. When the women began the project, they had decided that only those who were involved in the work would share in the produce or any potential income from sales. Since most of the hard work had already been completed, it seemed only fair to ask others to wait until it was time to begin work again on the next crop.

Local-brew club

Interest in the local-brew club planned in the August 1989 seminar dwindled to almost nothing as the women were preoccupied with the various intrigues surrounding the vegetable garden. Many of the men in the village actually tried to discourage the whole idea. In August 1990, during the participatory evaluation meeting, the men in attendance were very vocal in their disapproval of the project. They said that they thought it to be beyond the women's capabilities to manage.

When the women met in their small team for identifying new projects, they said that the men had other reasons for opposing the local-brew club. The women thought the men feared that if Managhat women organised a club, then the women would limit operating hours and limit the amount of drink prepared and sold; the men resented the prospect of wives and neighbouring women exercising so much control over their drinking habits. The women decided that it was not worth the trouble to fight over the issue if the men were so strongly united against the idea. The project was changed to establishing a "tea room" for women. This change was enthusiastically received by the' men when the proposal was reported back in the plenary session.

Later in the year as the women worked on the vegetable nursery and were caught up in the reorganisation of the UWT, the tea club dropped from their minds. No further interest was expressed in the project during the MAP monitoring interviews conducted in March and August 1991.

Other activities

Other development activities that emerged in Managhat during the two years of MAP monitoring were all the result of external intervention. As was seen above, Heifer Project International arrived in March 1990.

"Sasakawa Global 2000" initiated activities in Babati during the planting season in late 1990. This project sought to improve crop production. Managhat was one of many villages to receive training in new methods of raising maize. In addition to the training meetings, Global 2000 provided hybrid seed and fertilizer for a one-acre demonstration plot. The village government planted this acre and cared for it as a part of the 60-acre village farm.

Also mentioned above was the opportunity to send 15 village farmers to the "Rural Development Training Centre" in Monduli. This programme is sponsored by the Ministry of Livestock and Agriculture and every year two villages in the district are selected to send a group of representatives. Managhat was selected in 1991 because of its good progress in development activities. Fifteen participants from Managhat attended the programme during the month of April 1991.

FAO assisted a number of villages in Babati in building demonstration storage silos in 1991. Eleven of these were built in Managhat in July. FAO provided a bag of concrete and technical expertise for each silo as recipient farmers contributed the labour and other materials.

Endabeg Village Case Study

The village of Endabeg is located 14 kilometres west of Babati town and was originally registered in 1977. The population is very stable and only grew in number by five from 2,588 to 2,593 between August 1989 and August 1991..

Farming is the primary economic activity in Endabeg. The major crops are maize, beans, and pigeon peas. No grade cattle are kept in the village. During the course of the evaluation, the membership of the primary cooperative society shrank from 312 members to 223. This decline in membership mirrors a drop in total produce marketed through the society: 182,363 kgs of maize were sold through the cooperative in 1989 compared to only 47,910 kgs in 1990. The drop was because Endabeg farmers began to sell maize directly to the national milling company and does not imply a decrease in production. No records other than those of the co-op were maintained.

Facilities owned by the village government include a tractor, a maize-milling machine, and a small consumer shop. The co-op society also has a small consumer shop. The village tractor is the only one in Endabeg and is available for private hire. Only three farmers, however, hired the tractor in 1989. A tree nursery was established in late 1989 by the village government and distributes seedlings to farmers for a small price. An elementary school and a small dispensary are also located in the village. The village operated a farm of one hundred acres for generating money for the local government budget.

Discussions and Plans from the MAP Seminar

The seminar took place on the 23-24 August 1989 with 18 women and 27 men in attendance and was conducted at the village's CCM party office.

Vision items suggested by the women included an expansion of the local dispensary, clean water, construction of a small bridge on the footpath to Babati, and a vegetable and fruit nursery. The men also mentioned the building of a small bridge and a project for clean water. Additional suggestions from the men included a cattle dip, introduction of grade cattle, and the construction of a godown (i.e. storage shed).

During the question and answer period, the men asked the women to clarify many of their suggestions. The women explained that their major desire for the future was to see the construction of a new maternity room at the dispensary. They wanted a safe place where village women could go for the delivery of babies. When asked if the nursery they proposed was for the whole village or not, the women said it would benefit the whole village but they hoped to control it themselves.

The women in turn asked about the real prospects for a clean-water project. They had heard such promises before but nothing had come of it in the past. With great interest they learned about a missionary group that was proposing to run water-pipes through Endabeg to their facilities in a neighbouring village. If Endabeg could match Tsh. 120,000 from the missionaries, taps could be constructed in Endabeg itself.

The **obstacles** discussion was very limited and consisted primarily of laments from both the men and women on the lack of expertise in doing local projects. People complained that they were not receiving the governmental extension services due to them as were other villages in the district. Many of the suggestions that came from the **proposals** workshop concerned ways to ensure that extension officers would come more regularly to Endabeg.

On the second day of the workshop, **self-help projects** were planned for the coming year. In order to raise money for constructing a maternity room at the dispensary, the women proposed to start a 15 acre collective farm. The money from the sale of the produce would then be used to purchase timbers, roofing material, and furniture. They also proposed to start a vegetable garden and nursery. The two projects proposed by the men were the re-establishment of the village tree nursery and the construction of a new tea house.

The women's desire to start a farm aroused a lot of controversy. Upon reporting their plans they were immediately asked by the village chairman how they hoped to obtain land for starting a farm. The women said they thought the village council should allocate them 15-acres from the village government's own farm of 100 acres.

This was strongly resisted by the representatives of the council, all of whom were men, and a long discussion ensued during which the women continued to reiterate their demand for land. At one point the chairman said he could not understand why the women thought obtaining 15 acres was so important since the women would be required to work on the very same acres anyway even if they remained a part of the village farm. The women replied that they wanted the 15 acres so they could **control** the income and direct it toward their own priorities, especially building a maternity room at the dispensary.

Finally, the chairman suggested that the village government might consider designating 15 acres to the women if they proved themselves to be serious in their commitment. He did not want to designate land and then have it go unused. If the women could organise and register a local UWT club, something which the women in Endabeg had never done before, then fifteen acres would be set aside for the new club. After this long and emotional discussion about a women's farm, the other proposed self-help projects received little discussion and were generally approved.

Developmental Process of the Projects

Formation of a village UWT club

Though the village was registered in 1977, a local UWT club was never organised. Ten women in Endabeg had decided to become individual members of UWT due to their own particular circumstances but no club had ever been formed because no one had seen a reason to do so in the past.

The wife of the local Pentecostal pastor, for example, joined the UWT in 1970. She kept her membership active even after moving to Endabeg because it complemented her interest in church activities. Currently she serves as the nationally elected "Tanzanian Lay Leader for Pentecostal Women," a position which requires her to travel extensively over the country.

The pastor's wife had tried to organise a UWT club in Endabeg in 1984 but found no interest among other women. In fact, all of her organising effort with the women in Endabeg had ended in failure. She was, therefore, both delighted and surprised when she heard that the women were forming a UWT club and starting two special projects: the farm and a horticultural garden for vegetables.

The Endabeg UWT club was formally registered on 2 April 1990 with a total membership of 45. Eighteen other women had applied to join the club at that time but were forced to wait before having their names added to the rolls because only 45 membership cards had been sent to Endabeg from the district UWT office.

Launching of the women's farm

As the women progressed toward organising the UWT club, the village government designated nine acres of the village farm, instead of the promised fifteen, for the women's use. A work-day was organised by the women and four of these acres were prepared for cultivation and an application was made for the village tractor to do the work. This request was approved but the women were told that they would have to wait in a queue: cultivation of two farms belonging to the village government and the youth club had first to be completed before the tractor would be diverted to their project.

On 20 March 1990 the village tractor appeared to plough the women's four acres. This was in the middle of intense rains that resulted in extensive flooding across the district. Almost immediately upon entering the women's field, the tractor became stuck in the mud and could not move. The fields remained flooded for several more weeks as the rains continued to fall. By the time the tractor was freed and the women were able to give further attention to the farm, it was too late to plant a crop. The women decided to wait until the following year to start their farm.

In March 1991 the women repeated the same pattern established the year before. They prepared four acres by hand and requested use of the tractor for cultivation and planting. They collected 4,000 shillings and gave it to the village government to purchase fuel for the tractor. Once again the women were forced to wait for the tractor until all work was finished in the fields belonging to the village government and youth. When the tractor finally arrived, less than one acre of the women's farm was ploughed before the tractor was brought to a standstill with a punctured tyre.

When the tyre was finally repaired and the tractor began work again, the planting season was rapidly nearing its end. Then the tractor broke down yet again, this time with a hydraulic problem which would not be repaired for months to come. With one and half acres ploughed, the women were unable to plant a crop and postponed further work on their farm for one more year. This was the status of the women's farm at the end of the MAP monitoring period in August 1991.

Vegetable garden

The women were interested in starting a group vegetable garden primarily because they wished to improve the nutritional value of their meals at home. Surplus vegetables would be sold and the money applied to the women's fund, but income-generation was not a fundamental intention of the garden.

The biggest issue the women faced in starting their garden was obtaining an appropriate piece of land. The vegetables would require watering on a daily basis so the garden had to be located near a dependable source of water.

The women met among themselves and after some investigation identified a small-one acre plot which was currently lying fallow near the stream that runs through Endabeg. They met the owner of this plot in October 1989 and requested that he allow them to use the plot on a temporary basis so they could start their garden.

Their request was refused. Two years earlier the old mzee had allowed the current village chairman to use some of his land "on a temporary basis." But when he asked for it to be returned, the chairman refused. This issue was eventually taken to court and the old man lost control of the land to the chairman. Therefore, he did not wish to risk losing more of his land.

Progress on the vegetable garden ceased until the participatory evaluation meeting held in August 1990. In those discussions another location near the stream was proposed. Subsequent efforts to start the garden were frustrated, however, when the agricultural extension officer responsible for Endabeg stopped work on the garden saying that it was too close to a growing gully that was becoming an increasingly big environmental problem for the village.

Later in the year, the old *mzee* was again approached by women on an individual basis and asked if he would reconsider allowing them to use some of his land for personal gardens. This time, in exchange for a small amount of money, he agreed to do so. The chairperson of the Endabeg UWT obtained a small plot in this manner. By the time of the MAP project's final monitoring visit to Endabeg in August 1991, the women had renewed hopes of establishing their garden on an acre land because of the owner's new willingness to grant use to individuals. No agreement with the UWT, however, had yet been concluded.

Re-establishment of the village tree nursery

A tree nursery was originally established in Endabeg in 1985 when the village sent one man to a short course to learn about the care of young tree seedlings. The nursery thereafter received little attention from the village leadership and fell into disuse.

Renewed interest in Endabeg for tree planting had been slowly developing again according to the nursery caretaker, when the seminar was held in August 1989. In the preceding year, 1988, nearly 2,000 seedlings had been grown in the nursery and distributed to village farmers. During the seminar, plans were made to dramatically increase the number of seedlings produced in the nursery.

Following the seminar, work-days were organised as each sub-division within the village sent a delegation to work in the nursery. Sixty-five people were involved in these activities along with an entire class from the elementary school. This resulted in 10,340 seedlings being planted, an increase by five-fold from the previous year.

Once the seedlings matured, they were distributed to every household within the village in January 1990. Each household received ten to twenty seedlings which were then planted for future needs of timber, firewood, and fruit. While these plants were distributed free of charge in Endabeg, similar seedlings sold for twenty shillings each in Babati town. This may account for why 135 plants were stolen from the nursery prior to their distribution in the village.

Village ambitions for the tree nursery were very high at the beginning of 1990. The village council budgeted money for 22,600 seedlings which would allow the anticipated allocation of plants for each family to rise to over 30.

The nursery, however, fared less well than had been expected. Only 2,000 seedlings had been planted when the coordinator for the tree nursery fell ill. He then spent the next four months in the hospital. The nursery was poorly attended during his absence. When he finally returned in November 1990 he found that 620 seedlings had been stolen and that only 580 remained alive.

Approximately 800 plants had died. He also found that because so many of the seedlings had been stolen in his absence, the village council decided to move the nursery to an area nearby the party headquarters away from its previous location near his own farm.

In 1991, plans once again called for planting 20,000 seedlings. Just over 5,000 were actually planted when MAP stopped monitoring Endabeg in August. The village chairman explained that this disappointing number was largely due to the fact that the project coordinator now had to walk a long distance each day to attend to the seedlings.

Construction of a teahouse

The purpose of the teahouse was twofold. First, it would provide a place for villagers to come and socialise with one another in a casual and comfortable atmosphere and thereby serve as an alternative to the local-brew clubs. Second, it would provide a source of income for village projects. The priority among these projects was the installation of taps along the piped water going to the missionary project in the neighbouring village.

The idea of building a teahouse had been present in Endabeg for a long time prior to the holding of the seminar in August 1989, but the collective discussions of the seminar provided the immediate impetus to get started. This project was planned as a village-council project. Its implementation, therefore, followed a more formal approach with a works committee presenting plans and occasionally hiring skilled personnel from the village to do the work. By March 1990 the foundation had been dug and 2,000 bricks had been made and delivered to the construction site which was located immediately between the party headquarters and the maize mill.

By the time of the participatory evaluation meeting in August 1990, construction of the walls had been begun by a local village contractor who was paid 17,000 shillings to do the work. In February 1991, these walls were near completion. Used metal roofing-sheets from another building owned by the village council had been assigned for the teahouse and it was anticipated that they would soon be moved to the site.

The moving of the metal sheets had not yet happened by the final monitoring visit by the MAP project in August 1991. Though the village council had possession of the roofing material, it did not have timbers to serve as rafters for the roof. The village government was planning to use profits from the sale of pigeon peas from the council farm to purchase the rafters in October.

The strong desire to have a new maternity room at the local dispensary was the original motivating factor behind much of the women's activities in Endabeg. They formed a UWT club in order to obtain 15 acres of land for their own farm. They wanted the farm so they could control the income from produce sales to construct a maternity room. This remained the motivating factor behind the farm in March 1990. During the participatory evaluation meeting in August 1990, the women restated their ultimate desire to build a maternity room.

When the MAP project returned for its next monitoring visit in March 1991, the maternity room as a motivating factor had begun to shift. The Lutheran Dioceses which operated the current dispensary decided to construct an entirely new building. When the new building was completed, the Lutherans would return the existing facilities back to the village council. Upon learning about the Lutherans' plans, the village council decided that the vacated premises should be made into a maternity centre.

In August 1991 during the MAP last monitoring visit, the situation had shifted again. The final plans for the new Lutheran dispensary included a whole "maternity ward": a registration room, an examination room, a delivery room, and a recovery room. A Babati construction company had been contracted by the Lutherans to start work on 4 September 1991.

This new development meant that the maternity room was no longer a driving force behind the women's farm. Discussions with the Endabeg UWT leadership indicated that they still wanted to continue with the farm but that the income would be redirected to other projects which were as of that time still unnamed.

Interpretation of the Participatory Process

Four observations can be made about the activities that occurred after the completion of the MAP seminars. In some circumstances the seminars served as a stimulant for totally new activities; in others the seminars reinforced and accelerated existing ideas that were within the community even before the seminars were held; in some cases the seminar had no apparent influence at all on either a new or an existing project idea; and in some situations new activities which were completely unanticipated during the seminars arose at a later date. While some of these unanticipated activities benefited from the participatory environment that emerged from the seminars, others did not.

The MAP seminars apparently served as an **initiating stimulant** for the launching of Managhat's project for modern livestock keeping as well as for the formation of the UWT club in Endabeg and its attempts to start a women's farm.

Very little organised attention had been given to encouraging an expansion in the keeping of grade cattle in Managhat prior to the MAP seminar. An occasional individual reported that they had been considering the idea of keeping grade cows, but the seminar provided the major impetus for them to organise their efforts and to seriously investigate the realistic possibilities for taking up the practice. The two farmers interviewed during the monitoring exercise who already possessed grade dairy cows both expressed their surprise at the sudden interest that seemed to burst forth about their cows immediately after the seminar.

The formation of the UWT club in Endabeg and the subsequent attempts to establish a women's farm as an income-generating project were both ideas that had their genesis in the MAP seminar. Feeble efforts had been made many years earlier to form a UWT club, but the idea had long ago become nearly forgotten. It re-emerged in the seminar as a challenge to the women from the village chairman.

Many of the projects planned in the MAP seminars had been discussed within the villages in some form or another for a long time. The planning exercise in the seminars **reinforced and accelerated existing project ideas**. As was repeated in many of the interviews, ideas for many of the projects had been around for a long time: the seminars, however, provided an important boost to transforming such discussions into reality.

Both of the water projects in Managhat and Endabeg had been planned for a long time. The seminars enabled a renewed emphasis on their follow-up to occur. This was particularly true in Managhat where the district water engineer was contacted and new plans were drawn. Managhat also made a formal application to the Community Development Trust Fund for securing future funds. These follow-up activities in Managhat both took place immediately, i.e. the very next day, after the original seminar and the participatory evaluation meeting of a year later.

Collective vegetable gardens were also ideas that had been discussed by women in the two villages for a long time. The planning process in the seminars resulted in these ideas being translated into specific action. Progress was slow in coming, but some steps toward their eventual realisation were taken. By the end of the monitoring work of the MAP Project, the women of Managhat had succeeded in planting a small field of chinese cabbage; women in Endabeg re-initiated their search for securing an appropriate area for establishing their small horticulture project.

The idea of constructing a new teahouse in Endabeg was reportedly an idea that had been discussed by the village government on and off again for many years. The planning seminar enabled a firm decision to be reached and implementation work to begin within a very short period of time. Bricks were to go up within a year. The walls were completed and roofing material secured when the MAP monitoring exercise ended. Though some might view this progress as slow, it nevertheless remained a steady progress for a project that had previously been nothing but a wishful idea.

A need for a special maternity room at the local dispensary was clearly an idea that had been discussed by women in Endabeg prior to the seminar. Plans made during the seminar allowed them to take concrete steps toward realising their dream by forming the UWT club and attempting to start their own income-producing farm. The fact that the farm was unable to become functional within the two-year period or that the Lutheran Diocese planned to provide them with a new maternity centre does not negate the fact that the seminar enabled the women to take practical action in an organised manner for the first time.

In some circumstances, **the seminar had no apparent influence** on the implementation of projects planned in the group discussions. This was true for some old established projects in the village and with newly suggested projects.

This was particularly the case with the village farms operated by the village governments. Both Managhat and Endabeg designated income from the farms during the seminars in support of the new water projects. In both cases, there was no discernible difference in the production of the farms while the incomes were in actuality used for other more immediate needs than the water projects, especially the repair of the village tractors.

The women in Managhat planned to establish a local-brew club. When the men objected to the club, this project proposal was changed in the participatory evaluation meeting one year after the seminar to a teahouse. This was an empty gesture that finally came to nothing as no action whatsoever was ever taken on the project.

A few **unanticipated activities** which had never been discussed emerged after the seminars. These were all the result of unexpected opportunities that arose when external agencies arrived with gifts in some form for the villages.

Heifer Project International came to Managhat with a proposal to provide ten farmers with grade cows. Because this proposal so closely matched a major priority activity planned during the seminar, interest in HPI was high and progress with the project proceeded at a fast pace. FAO silos and the demonstration acre of maize supported by Global 2000 were introduced to a large number of villages in the district, including Managhat. The opportunity to send Managhat villagers to the Rural Development Training Centre in 1991 was a special opportunity since only one village a year is invited to do so in Babati.

The decision by the Lutheran Diocese to include a maternity centre in their new dispensary came as a complete surprise to villagers in Endabeg. Though community residents were not involved in formulating plans or making decisions about the new dispensary, the local director of the dispensary was present at the original seminar and observed the women making their strong pleas with the village government for the opportunity to manage a farm so that income could be used to establish a maternity room.

Causal Relationships

The Endabeg and Managhat case studies earlier in the chapter describe activities that took place after the completion of MAP seminars in each village. One question, however, immediately springs to mind when considering MAP: would those activities have been likely to occur in any case even without the intervention of the seminars?

Many of those interviewed from the villages attributed much, if not most, of the progress with local projects to the planning discussions from the seminar. Yet the interviews also revealed that there were many other factors that came into play with much of the project implementation.

The promise of heifer cows from HPI was obviously the major factor in the resulting activities that took place within the Managhat livestock-keeping project. Farmers planted small pastures for zero-grazing and built sheds for sheltering the cattle because it was a direct requirement from HPI before any farmer could receive a gift cow. The initial receptivity and enthusiasm of the Managhat farmers for entering into these activities, however, was strongly connected to plans made during the seminar to embark upon a project for modern livestock keeping within the village.

In the 1989 seminar, women planned to start a collective horticultural project through the launching of a small vegetable garden. Several problems and false starts forced long delays before a half acre of chinese cabbage was planted nearly two years after the project was originally planned. The successful planting of the vegetable garden coincided with the return of two women from the programme at the Rural Development Training Centre in Monduli.

It is obvious that the training programme at RDTC, the initiation of the HPI project, and the MAP seminars were all contributing factors to the successful implementation of these projects. It is difficult to conclude, however, that any of one them was the key determining factor over the others. Proof of a simple cause and effect relationship could not be found in the monitoring exercise. A review of the evidence does suggest that the planning seminars and subsequent follow-up work in Managhat and Endabeg played an important **catalytic role** in enabling the process of self-reliant development to occur.

Continuing Problems with Participatory Projects

The MAP seminars and various interventions from other projects could not, of course, enable villagers to overcome all of their problems. At the end of the two-year monitoring exercise several problems continued to hamper the successful conclusion of many local projects.

For two years running, the women of Endabeg were forced to be last in the queue for use of the village tractor in cultivating their farm. In both years the women were unable to plant a crop. There is little to indicate that this pattern will not continue for the next year. One cannot help but wonder how long can the women be frustrated in their activities before they stop work altogether. This is especially true since the primary motivation of their work, the establishment of a maternity room, is no longer a pressing concern due to an expansion of the dispensary by the Lutherans.

By the end of the MAP monitoring period, the Endabeg women had still been unable to secure land for their proposed vegetable garden. Though the project was still being pursued, the outcome was very uncertain. The big issue with the Managhat vegetable garden was creating the practical means, and perhaps the will, for opening the project for broader participation by other women in the community.

Both water projects in Managhat and Endabeg remained dependent upon requests for external funding. If the funding is not forthcoming, it is very doubtful that either community will make additional progress in implementing their water projects.

Comparison of Results

Because of the unique conditions that exist for each village and for each project, it is very difficult to compare results from Endabeg or Managhat to those of another village. No control village is, therefore, really possible for comparing results from the MAP seminars. Still, it is interesting to make comparisons where possible with other villages. Then, too, activities within a village after a seminar can be compared with activities that took place before it was held.

The HPI officer responsible for the Babati District reported that Managhat was the most active and enthusiastic of all the villages with which he had worked. He compared Managhat with the neighbouring village of Singe, which was scheduled to receive ten cows at the same time that Managhat was to receive ten cows, and with two other villages that had received HPI cows in the preceding years. According to him, Managhat was far better organised and prepared to implement HPI requirements than any of the other three villages. Singe was so far behind in this work that when the cows were finally distributed by HPI, 19 went to Managhat farmers and only one to a Singe farmer instead of the original ten to each village.

Though the women of Endabeg were frustrated in much of their development work, the intensity of their activities after the MAP seminar was dramatically greater than anything they had ever done before. The formation of the UWT club, the attempts to plant the farm, and the unsuccessful search for securing land for a vegetable garden showed a significant increase in activities from the preceding years.

The villagers of Managhat and Endabeg who were interviewed during the course of the monitoring exercise insisted that they were able to make such progress in comparison to other villages and their own past performance because of discussions and the making of plans during the MAP seminar.

Conclusions

Quantifiable methods are of limited value in evaluating the results from participation promotional activities like the MAP seminars. Qualitative methods allow for an evaluator to discern patterns within local communities that better explain the participatory processes that are released in such seminars.

Monitoring work in the villages of Managhat and Endabeg found that the seminars did play an important catalytic role in the two communities. In many cases the seminar stimulated totally new initiatives that had not ever been broadly considered before. More often, the seminars enabled villagers to take existing ideas and to accelerate implementation activities and move them toward completion. In a few instances projects were discussed that were controversial, like the local-brew club in Managhat, and were totally ignored after the completion of the seminar.

The seminars assisted the villages to clarify their plans and prepared them to take immediate advantage of new opportunities as they arose. Because Managhat had already decided that it needed to encourage the keeping of grade cows and had organised itself to seek ways of doing this, it was ready to respond seriously to the Heifer Project.

Some projects are too big to be accomplished solely on a self-help basis. This was true of the water projects in both villages. Though the seminars helped remind the villages of their keen interest in water development and catalysed the preparation and submission of proposals to different funding agencies, ultimate results will depend upon the arrival of external financial inputs. The limitations of a self-help approach were thereby reached with these projects.

Chapter 7

MAP IN COMPARISON WITH OTHER PARTICIPATORY APPROACHES

The design of a participation promotion programme involves a number of strategic decisions. As has been demonstrated in the preceding chapters, the flexibility of MAP has allowed it to be adapted to the needs of many different types of programmes and developmental situations.

MAP, of course, has not been alone in developing participatory methodology. This chapter examines some of the other programmes that have gained a degree of notoriety in regard to participation. These programmes are not an exhaustive list, but they do illustrate some of the broad trends and approaches to participatory development that are popular today. "Rapid Rural Appraisal" (RRA) is considered in the light of participatory consultations with large development schemes and programmes. The "People's Participation Programme" (PPP) places a major emphasis on small group formation. "Training for Transformation" (TFT) is a programme largely inspired by the writings of Paulo Freire. The "Community Development Trust Fund" of Tanzania (CDTF) is only one of many programmes that encourage . participation through the donation of money or materials to local projects.

"Rapid Rural Appraisal" and Consultations

"Rapid Rural Appraisal" is a relatively new approach to conducting action-oriented research in developing countries and was pioneered by the Institute of Development Studies at the University of Sussex. As an approach, it is oriented toward large development projects. It makes use of multi-disciplinary teams to develop quick yet systematic research findings, with much of its success dependent upon direct contact with community leaders. Hypotheses can be formulated and tested in a very brief time, perhaps only two or three weeks, in comparison to many months or years for more traditional approaches to research.

RRA as Practised by the IIED

The International Institute for Environment and Development (IIED) has done extensive work in developing RRA methods for agricultural development. It describes four classes of RRA methodologies.

"**Exploratory RRAs** are used in the early stages of project planning to produce preliminary hypotheses for later testing by development work or further research. **Topical RRAs** are used to answer a specific key question. The question may have been asked by a previous exploratory RRA or may come from local research or extension workers. **Participatory RRAs** are used to help involve farming households in all stages of development work, from the identification of needs to the assessment of completed projects. **Monitoring RRAs** are used to evaluate the success and impact of development activities, whether these are products of an RRA or a more conventional planning process" (McCracken, Pretty, Conway; p. 3).

RRA is adaptable to the specific needs of different projects. It uses a number of participatory techniques in its research undertakings, but in a sense RRA itself remains "contentless." It plays a secondary supporting role to the purposes of a primary project and is, therefore, instrumentally tied to the ultimate aims, objectives, and design of the particular project with which it is being used.

Core techniques for RRA described by the IIED are secondary data review, direct observation, semi-structured interviews, analytical games, stories and portraits, diagrams, and workshops. The participatory nature of these techniques involve not only the collection of the information with local people but structured feedback on preliminary findings. The RRA techniques "are based on very close relationship between professionals and farmers and can only really be undertaken on a small and intimate scale".

Participatory Consultations

Development intervention by governments and agencies have primarily taken the form of relatively large-scale "projects" that are usually related to a specific sector of activity. Popular participation is increasingly recognised as a means of acquiring and utilising local knowledge and ensuring the long-term "sustainability" of the project. This often takes the form of involving local residents in aspects of project planning, implementation, and evaluation.

RRA is only one of many approaches to develop practical methodologies for involving people in participatory consultations. The Development Studies Unit of the Department of Social Anthropology at the University of Stockholm has developed a series of "guidelines" and "fieldwork methods" for such consultations that are similar to many of those found within RRA.

The Development Studies Unit has put these to the test in different field situations. In one of these it worked with the "Kwale Water and Sanitation Project" (KWSP) in Kenya for ten days in November 1990 (Rudqvist and Tobisson). This consultation resulted in "directly and indirectly project related problems" and "project/community opportunities" that emerged from a series of interviews and group meetings. The insights gained from these participatory encounters were then incorporated by the staff of KWSP into the future activities of the project.

MAP as a Consultation Method

The Babati Land Management Programme has been the primary field application of MAP for enabling participation in the planning of large-scale projects. That work, as explained in Chapter 4, consisted of two phases. In the first, village participants in four pilot villages planned local projects that they could do on their own resources independent of LAMP. Two external consultants who were participant observers in all of the planning sessions (in this case, the MAP researchers) then made a series of proposals for the future of LAMP operations based on the workshop proceedings.

The second-phase "constituency" seminars with contending interest groups (pastoralists, small subsistence farmers, large commercial farmers, and district officials) was intended to provide a more direct planning input into future LAMP projects than were the first-phase seminars with pilot villages. Operational problems, however, forced LAMP to delay the constituency seminars until after many projects were well under way. Though successful completion of both phases as originally intended would have undoubtedly been more effective, MAP was able to assist LAMP in the planning of district projects responsive to local needs.

The MAP approach with LAMP differs from many other similar participatory consultations in one major regard. Rather than merely seeking information from grassroots residents as an input into the planning of big projects, MAP placed an immediate emphasis on self-reliant development. The focus of each seminar was the planning of local self-help projects; village participants were constantly considering the initiatives for which they themselves needed to assume total responsibility. The resulting "input" into LAMP planning process was an indirect by-product of the seminars.

Other participatory consultations may intend to encourage eventual involvement by local residents in implementation activities, but this is often slow in coming as project officers hammer out the details of proposed projects.

"People's Participation Programme" and Small Group Formation

The People's Participation Programme (PPP) of the UN's Food and Agriculture Organisation (FAO) operates in eight African nations including Tanzania, Kenya, and Zambia. PPP is perhaps one of the most publicized participation programmes currently operating in Africa. It, therefore, demands attention in any discussion about participatory methodology.

Though FAO provides general assistance to national PPP projects, each project is accomplished through different implementing organisations funded by various donors. FAO assistance includes consultations on project design, training of animators, and project monitoring and evaluation. The Cooperative College is the implementing body in Tanzania and the Ministry of Agriculture and Water Development is in Zambia. A non-governmental organisation (NGO), Partnership for Productivity, serves as the implementing body in Kenya. The government of the Netherlands provides funding for each of these three national projects.

The PPP Programme in Practice

PPP seeks to empower the more marginalized members of the rural population through working with small homogeneous groups of no more than ten people. Animators, or "group promoters," are employed by the national implementing organisation and live in the villages where they work. In Tanzania, a man and a woman work as an animation team in each village. They spend their initial time meeting with the poorer members of the community, informally discussing with them problems that they face and possible solutions. During this time, animators are trying to identify natural groupings of eight to fifteen people who might work together in small capital-formation projects for enhancing personal incomes. This process of identifying groups, naming problems, and planning projects might take up a full year to complete.

Animators maintain regular contact with these village groups following the initiation of projects. This support continues for two years. Group promoters assist the groups in small ways, helping them to overcome problems as they arise. This often calls for the group promoters to play a mediating role with government agencies or other organisations.

A major component of the PPP approach is enabling these small groups to gain access to credit on favourable terms. Part of the national coordination of PPP entails enlisting a national lending institution to provide loans which in turn are secured by a "guarantee-cum-risk fund" set up by PPP (FAO; Huizer; Kibwana; van Heck).

Small Group Formation

Like PPP, many other contemporary participation programmes are concerned with the formation of small homogeneous groups for enhancing individual incomes. Because of their emphasis on grassroots mobilisation, the unique features of these programmes are particularly interesting in a discussion about MAP. Below are a few additional examples of such approaches.

"Planning Rural Development at the Village Level" (PRD) in Tanzania is a pilot programme supported by UNICEF. In a very similar design to the PPP, PRD animators focus on identifying and forming small groups within a village to encourage group activities for capital formation. As with the PPP, the process of forming these groups might take as long as one year to accomplish. PRD animators also take up residence in the communities where they work; they are expected to play an intermediary role between the small groups that they form and outside agencies and government structures.

To date PRD has provided no access to favourable credit, though it is the intention in the very near future to secure such a service through PRD activities (UNICEF, 1987). PRD also has intentions of training local residents as "auxiliary" animators who will play an increasing role in sustaining project activities. This will lighten the responsibilities placed on the PRD animators who will then be able to expand their work to surrounding villages (Tilakaratna; Jonsson, et al.).

Koenraad Verhagen has worked extensively with "Self-Help Organisations" (SHO). His written work draws upon experiences in two related action-research projects on self-help promotion in a controlled number of villages in Brazil, Sri Lanka, and Thailand (Verhagen 1984, 1987). The purpose of this research, particularly of that in 1984, was to experiment with the development of a methodology for promoting informal "cooperation" groups parallel to (but also with the implicit approval of) formally registered "cooperatives." This research work was sanctioned by the International Cooperative Alliance.

The focus of the SHO research called for "change agents," who were development professionals and did not reside in the communities, to work with the poorest members of the population in the villages. "Action-Researchers," or change agents, "acted not only as researchers, but also as organisers of group discussions, planners, trainers, advisors and, to some extent, as 'expressive leaders'" (Verhagen 1984, p. 170). An expressive leader "is someone who can mobilise and stimulate the group and can convince it that the stated objective can be realised" (Verhagen 1984, p.111).

The change agents began by conducting household surveys to identify the target population and potential self-help groups. Though size was a flexible matter, groups were only formed with people who considered each other to be peers; the "better-off" farmers were not mixed with the poorer farmers. Strict criteria were used for determining which farmers fell into these categories. "Participatory research and planning" followed the completion of the surveys. Over a three to four-month period, several meetings and informal discussions took place within the groups and finally culminated in the planning of self-help "micro-projects." Most of the projects undertaken by these groups tended to be ones that generated income for group members.

Material or financial assistance was not a part of the projects, though that possibility was held open for the future; the research report expressed deep reservations about the benefits of "cheap credit":

"The availability of external credit disorients the groups; it changes their orientation. Instead of searching for ways and means to mobilise or generate financial resources by their own efforts, small farmers tend to make themselves dependent, as a group or individuals, on the credit facilities offered by the bank or the Project" (Verhagen 1984, p. 155).

Change agents did play a "linking" role with third parties and were involved in education and training for group members. They also provided different forms of "management consultancy" to the groups and assisted in monitoring and on-going evaluation of the group's work. When the research project came to an end, groups continued with their own projects on their own. A final product of the research with SHO was the creation of a "Plan of Action" on how formal cooperative structures may support the SHO cooperation groups in the future. Verhagen's further research-work systematized this into the identification of eight instruments for supporting grassroots development (Verhagen 1984; 1987).

MAP and the Formation of Small Groups

Most adaptations of MAP have attempted to have seminar participants selected in a manner that is representative of the rural community as a whole. Strict homogeneity of small groups has not been a priority concern as it has with other programmes described above.

This is not to say that MAP adaptations have naively treated rural communities as homogeneous entities. Distinct and conflicting interests are to be found in every village. Women in particular often have different views and concerns from men. By having participants who represent all social and economic aspects of the village attend planning seminars, it is possible to give a voice to those who are often excluded.

CMPP in Kenya and Zambia limit invitations to those who are co-op members and the projects planned during the seminar are exclusively for the cooperative society. In contrast, participants in Tanzanian CMPP seminars include both members and non-members and project ownership is an open question. This way, CMPP in Tanzania fosters the creation of small groups that generally tend to be composed of people with similar backgrounds and who trust one another. Chapter 3 discussed the distinction between "grassroots mobilisation" and "institution strengthening" found in CMPP.

CMPP, especially in Kenya and Zambia, does not directly address the issue of capital formation and income enhancement for individuals. CMPP basically attempts to empower the existing cooperative structures in those countries and hopes to make them more sensitive to the needs of the poorer members of the area. Most projects planned during CMPP in Kenya and Zambia share a strong similarity to traditional community development projects in that they are intended for the general benefit of the community as a whole.

The unique dimension of CMPP in Tanzania for small group ownership of projects lends itself more easily towards the prospect of capital formation and personal income enhancement. Trust, accountability, and control of decisions are much more likely to occur in small homogeneous groups than in larger bodies, as PPP and others have strongly argued. These crucial factors are clearly evident in Tanzania when CMPP projects are "owned" by small production groups, even though they are not formed in the same manner as the homogeneous groups of PPP or PRD.

All three national CMPPs are expansive in their strategy as they work with many communities across large areas of geography. Facilitators with CMPP spend much less time in close follow-up work with villages than do PPP group promoters who work intensely with only a very few communities or PRD where animators actually live in the village where they are engaged. Similarly, CMPP facilitators do not mediate on behalf of a village for technical or material resources from external agencies as do many other programmes.

One of the unique aspects of MAP is the highly structured two-day planning seminar which functions as the primary process for initiating group activities. PPP, PRD, and SHO all follow an approach that requires long extended periods of time in forming groups and launching activities. The "research and planning" phase, as one programme calls it, takes many months to complete and involves many meetings and informal conversations. The discussions in these meetings also tend to be very loosely structured affairs. This is in sharp contrast to the quick pace and tightly structured formats of MAP seminars.

"Training for Transformation" and Conscientization

"Training for Transformation" (TFT) is built directly on the conscientization principles of Paulo Freire and is based on a series of resource books written and published in Zimbabwe. These manuals present a flexible process which is often modified to local conditions by those attracted to the Freire approach. TFT uses simple methods of "education by discovery" through interactive learning. This places participants on centre stage rather than a teacher. It is a process of awareness training that seeks to awaken people to the structural causes of their problems. Loosely related TFT activities by many different groups and individuals can be found throughout east and central Africa. The description below is of the systematized TFT programme carried out by the Catholic Secretariat in Zambia.

"Training for Transformation" in Zambia

TFT in Zambia begins by having small groups of people who live in close geographical proximity to each other attend a regional training workshop. This lasts for a week and is led by trainers from the Secretariat who guide participants through a carefully prepared curriculum. Several questions are explored: what is development, what prevents development from happening, how can people effectively address these problems? Educational techniques in the "discovery" process include games, drama, role-play, art-forms, presentations, and discussions.

Participants are prepared to use these same methods of awareness training once they return to their home community. This includes the conducting of a community survey, which is a carefully orchestrated set of interviews and re-interviews which can take many months to complete. Action is planned around "burning issues," i.e. the big problems within the community as discerned by people in the long process of completing the survey. In practice, the resulting action-plans are seldom related to income generation; they often concern community-wide issues like health or education. Since the process is entirely open, the focus of any activities that might eventually be planned is totally dependent upon the issues identified by the general population.

The Secretariat continues to support these local initiatives by offering three follow-up workshops. Each lasts for a full week and all take place within the twelve-month period following the original workshop. These workshops provide support to groups leading the process in their home communities. Secretariat staff also make visits in the field to discuss progress and problems with these group leaders.

TFT is very much opposed to material or financial assistance to these groups from outside sources. Consistent with their use of simple, easy to convey messages, TFT calls this "spoon-feeding." TFT views this as having a pacifying effect because it creates a distraction from awakening people to the real structural causes of their poverty (Walsh; Hope & Timmel).

MAP and Conscientization

Conscientization refers to the process whereby the poor gain a greater sense of awareness about the structural causes of their poverty. This in turn leads to a better understanding of how those problems might be significantly addressed. The approach to community development work found in TFT gives a practical form to this type of "awareness training."

MAP shares many similarities with this basic approach. MAP seminars are open-ended affairs where people struggle to identify underlying obstacles that are frustrating the realisation of their vision for the future. Facilitators do not impose any particular solutions. These obstacles emerge from an interactive learning process as participants discuss their problems. They share their experiences with each other and draw up the deep insight of their collective "common sense."

Another similarity shared by TFT and many of the programmes employing MAP methods is an avoidance of providing material or financial assistance to community groups.

MAP differs considerably from TFT and other conscientization programmes in that it moves at a much quicker pace. TFT activities take months to complete in a community compared to the two-day seminar and quarterly follow-up meetings found with MAP.

"Community Development Trust Fund" and External Inputs

The "Community Development Trust Fund" (CDTF) is a Tanzanian programme for assisting community development projects; this is largely done through the provision of financial support. A community organisation can apply to CDTF for up to 60% of the costs involved for doing a small-scale project. CDTF maintains project officers in seven zones across the country.

These officers are available over long periods to help local leaders identify community needs and write project proposals to CDTF. They also receive grant applications, train local project leaders, and monitor overall project progress. Any community organisation or village government is eligible to apply for CDTF grants.

CDTF in Tanzania

When a project application is approved by CDTF, a "group leader" is selected from the local community to coordinate project activities. CDTF provides basic training for these leaders in simple project administration and bookkeeping and offers small incentives to keep them actively involved, e.g. allowances, a bicycle, training. All financial assistance from the CDTF is channelled through District Councils to the village organisations once a "site ledger" has been established for the project. Each of the seven zones has a Landrover and a lorry to provide logistical support in ferrying materials to project sites. CDTF can also provide "soft loans" to communities, but these must be secured by two guarantors. (see Pendaeli)

Support through the Donation of External Inputs

CDTF is typical of many donor-oriented organisations that are involved in field promotion of self-help activities. Activities of many well-known development organisations, e.g. "Save the Children" and "World Vision" to name just a couple, often attempt to stimulate self-help and self-reliance through the provision of material or financial grants. Such programme designs may vary considerably with other types of ongoing support (the presence of animators, training of local coordinators, etc.), but the provision of external financial or material resources in some form or another remains a constant aspect which binds the approaches of these programmes together.

Similarities and Difference with MAP and CDTF

One of the important similarities with programmes like CDTF and those programmes that have applied MAP is an expansive strategy to work with many communities at one time rather than with just a very few. A programme like CDTF does this by largely limiting its assistance to a financial grant while MAP does so by limiting its assistance to a planning process.

The particular means of assisting these communities is thereby that which distinguishes MAP from such programmes. In very few instances have MAP adaptations involved the provision of material or financial resources to village groups.

Conclusion

The consultation methods of "Rapid Rural Appraisal," the formation of small homogeneous groups for income generation, awareness training, and simple financial assistance are among the most common participation approaches practised today. Comparing them with MAP helps to clarify many of the unique features that comprise MAP methodology.

Chapter 8

OTHER ADAPTATIONS OF MAP

The MAP project was conceived as a research project for developing participatory methodology for use in rural development. CMPP, LAMP, and IRDP/EP all provided valuable field experience for adapting MAP for use in villages and with farmers of primary cooperative societies.

MAP, however, is a very flexible methodology that can be applied in many other circumstances outside of the confines of rural communities. This chapter briefly describes three adaptations of MAP beyond the rural countryside.

Agricultural Sector Planning Process in Zambia

The Agricultural Sector Support Programme (ASSP) has long been an important aspect of Swedish bilateral aid to Zambia. As the current ASSP comes to an end in 1992, it was decided jointly by SIDA and the Ministry of Agriculture during the ASSP Annual Review in October 1990 to initiate a new participatory planning process for formulating the future directions of Swedish support to Zambian agriculture. This has since become known as the "Agricultural Sector Planning Programme" (ASSP).

The participatory nature of this planning process was of particular interest because of the growing tendency for donors to become more and more involved in formulating programmes of development cooperation. The influence of donors is most often manifest in the work of expatriate consultants who submit proposals based on short-term field work. As the IRDC noted in its concept paper on ASPP, this tendency has created a number of problems. Donor priorities often become the basis of project planning instead of the ambitions and preferences of recipient countries. Relevant knowledge is often ignored because of limited involvement of local representatives. And perhaps the most important of all, the lack of involvement of recipient country representatives often results in a corresponding lack of commitment to implement projects (Birgegaard 1990).

The intent of the ASPP was to enable Zambian officials in the agriculture sector to play an essential role in formulating the future directions of Swedish support, thereby reversing the trend where assistance planning is dominated by expatriate consultants. The ASPP approach attempted to maintain four basic characteristics:

1) a leadership role of local staff
2) a wide participation in the analytical efforts
3) external (foreign) input limited primarily to a facilitating role
4) analytical process is de-linked from the donor to limit influence.

The International Rural Development Centre (IRDC) at the Swedish University of Agricultural Sciences in Uppsala played a facilitating role in enabling this process to take place. The IRDC in Uppsala invited the MAP Project to assist in **developing practical methodologies** for use in the ASPP and to assist in **facilitating the different workshops**. Senior government officials were obviously a far different audience from the cooperative members and grassroots villagers with whom the MAP had been typically working. Yet the participatory methodologies for "policy formation and project analysis" were not that far removed from those used in community planning of self-help projects. The basic elements of the process remained the same.

ASPP occurred within three agricultural sub-sectors: marketing and input supply, research and seed development, and institution building. Core groups, consisting of five to six people, were appointed by the Permanent Secretary of the Ministry of Agriculture to coordinate the planning of each sub-sector. All three sub-sectors followed a similar process. Key to this process was three different workshops which took place over a two to three-day period and were attended by a large number of project implementors.

The first was a "problems identification workshop" which occurred in January 1991. This was followed by the commissioning of in-depth studies in areas determined during the workshop and assigned to individuals or teams from among the workshop participants. Upon their completion, these studies were presented at a second "programme options workshop" in April where priorities were set. The core group then took the priorities and formulated programmes and projects which were then approved in a "programme selection workshop" in June 1991. The results of this workshop were then submitted to SIDA in anticipation of the ASSP Annual Review which occurred in August and September 1991 (Fones-Sundell, Erikson, and Berresford).

The results of the ASSP Annual Review called for 1992 to be a year for further developing the programmes that emerged from the six-month planning process facilitated by IRDC. Consultants in the Annual Review thought that particular attention needed to be given to clarifying the national policies of agricultural development that supported the proposals which emerged from the planning process. In the meantime, SIDA created a bridging year of financial support to Zambian agricultural development.

Institutional Strengthening Beyond the Rural Areas

The MAP Project has been interested in adapting participation approaches for use in different levels of the development establishment. The work with the ASPP in Zambia provided an opportunity to use MAP methods with a professional audience.

Within the cooperative movement, MAP planning would benefit all levels of its operation. If cooperative apex organisations were to utilise a MAP approach to planning, then a more participatory environment would be enhanced across the breadth of the movement and reinforce the efforts of CMPP in the primary societies. Though MAP did not succeed in its desire to so assist cooperative apex organisations, the ASPP with the Ministry of Agriculture fulfilled much of the same ambition.

Participatory planning is a means for strengthening institutions through practical improvements in an organisation's performance. Though it does not address the whole spectrum of institution building (e.g. technical training), participatory planning complements other efforts and renders many beneficial results:

- the formation of creative solutions and action-plans because those who have a stake and practical expertise in an organisation are brought together to discern new directions;

- greater ability to implement plans because people become more informed and involved through the planning process;

- more innovation because the cross-fertilization of different minds can more easily challenge traditional assumptions;

- greater teamwork and cooperation because a common framework for decision-making, communication, and problem–solving is created;

- the encouragement of initiative and responsibility because people feel a greater sense of commitment through ownership of the plan.

The flexibility of the MAP planning methodology can be adapted to meet the sophistication of any audience. Participatory planning can and should take place on a number of different levels because work at one level reinforces work in another: co-op apex organisations, regional unions, and primary societies; local development committees and district councils; the head offices for development assistance agencies and field implementation centres.

Participatory consultations can be a valuable means for "institution building" both with government bodies and indigenous NGOs in developing countries through other related topics. Strategic planning workshops are a common one, but organisational audits and needs assessments, programme evaluations, and "philosophy and mission" retreats are also valuable topics of consultations for strengthening the operations of many institutions.

Conference Facilitation

MAP methodologies were also applied during the course of the project in the holding of a number of conferences. Three different "participation forums" were conducted by MAP that brought together practitioners and academics to discuss current developments in participation. A similar conference was held for the "CMPP Regional Symposium."

Conferences differ from planning seminars in a number of ways. MAP seminars are aimed at creating practical plans with actual implementation steps for groups of people who work together as colleagues. They are responsible for carrying out a shared task of one form or another. Conferences, however, usually bring together a wide spectrum of delegates whose only common bond is a shared interest. Conference delegates are rarely engaged in the implementation of common tasks.

This places a different emphasis on the application of MAP methods in conference settings in a slightly different perspective, though the basic approach remains the same. The lively interaction of participants through the facilitation of discussions and workshops are in sharp contrast to the typical conference comprised of one speech after another.

MAP methods were developed for use in rural villages, but their applications are far broader. Institution building, conferences, and strategic planning workshops are three good examples.

Chapter 9

THE TRAINING OF MAP FACILITATORS

Facilitators play the most crucial role in any participation promotion programme because they are the ones who make the direct contact with the rural population. It is an unfamiliar role to most of those who are assigned the responsibilities of being a facilitator. The task of training personnel for this work is extremely important. This chapter begins with a look at the journey of becoming a facilitator. It then examines some of the major challenges confronting facilitators in their work: enabling high levels of participant involvement, ensuring high-quality thinking on the part of participants, and maintaining an effective sense of flexibility in follow-up work to seminars.

The Journey of Becoming a Facilitator

As can be seen in the experience of MAP adaptations, facilitators play an indispensable role in participation programmes. Their work-load is heavy as they make many field visits to societies. Yet, when all is said and done, they don't spend a great amount of time working within a single location. This makes the time they do spend in the field all the more important.

Facilitators guide the planning of self-help projects by asking questions and refraining from stating their own opinions or instructing participants in answers presumed to be correct. Facilitation is difficult because its style is contrary to much development work. Facilitators must break the conventional mould of a teacher or extension officer. Educators are often trapped by an "anti-participatory orientation" found in African schools (Bugnicourt) while extension officers regularly become "salesmen" hawking predetermined plans from a central development office (Timberlake). Neither serves as a good model for a facilitator. Facilitators challenge participants to draw conclusions based on their own experiences rather than propagate ready-made answers.

An established structure for each workshop is usually spelled out in great detail in a programme manual. Facilitators, however, cannot effectively lead discussions by merely following an instructions book. A facilitator must have the sensitivity to ask the right question at the right time to illuminate the issue under discussion. The degree to which MAP facilitators can do this job determines the success of a MAP seminar. The training of facilitators is one of the biggest issues facing any programme that uses MAP methods.

Facilitators do monitoring and follow-up with participants once a seminar is over, but they don't play a mediating role with outside agencies or authorities. If villagers need some technical assistance or information in implementing their projects, they organise themselves to get the job done. Mediation by a facilitator tends to undermine independence and self-confidence in the same way that premature introduction of capital inputs do: it can inadvertently foster dependency rather than self-reliance.

Selection of Facilitators

Different approaches have been utilised in selecting potential facilitators for the MAP-related programmes. CMPP in Kenya, Tanzania, and Zambia followed different models. In some instances facilitators have been recruited from the general public to work with CMPP on a full-time basis. In other situations, current cooperative extension officers and movement training officers add CMPP to their other on-going responsibilities.

Ten facilitators were hired for CMPP in Tanzania, each of whom responded to newspaper advertisements. The woman who currently serves as the national CMPP coordinator in Kenya responded to a similar advertisement in 1986. After a review of written applications, a short-list of potential candidates were interviewed for the positions. A number of important characteristics were sought in these interviews: personal interest in working with rural people, desire to assist in women's development, willingness to work for extended periods of time in rural areas, previous experience in mobilisation activities. A background in cooperative development, just in and of itself, was given a lower priority.

Except for the national coordinator, the other facilitators in Kenya are either extension officers working with the Ministry of Cooperative Development or "cooperative education and promotional officers" (CEPO) working with various district cooperative unions. The same is true for all CMPP facilitators in Zambia who were already government or union employees. When CMPP is introduced to a new area, these provincial or district cooperative personnel attend CMPP training seminars to prepare them for conducting the programme. Three phases of training usually occur and are described in the following sections.

There are three phases through which people pass on their journey to becoming capable MAP facilitators. First, novice facilitators learn the basics of MAP and are oriented to a participatory approach to group planning. They become acquainted with the intent, format, and logistics of the programme and become familiar enough to explain the purpose and design of MAP to others. At this point they spend time watching MAP seminars being conducted by experienced facilitators.

In the second phase of the journey, facilitators begin to put their theoretical ideas about MAP into practice. They actually stand before groups and lead seminar discussions. In the beginning they usually rely heavily upon the facilitator's guide which serves as a blueprint for the seminars. Very quickly, however, they find themselves no longer dependent upon the printed procedures and lead discussions from memory. Gradually, they do less of the talking in seminars and encourage participants to speak more. It is during this period that new facilitators begin to realise that their job is to ask questions and to refrain from supplying the answers.

These first two phases occur primarily by watching and conducting seminars. The longer they are involved in doing this, the more confident novice facilitators become as they grow familiar with the MAP routine: they follow the blueprint, ask the questions, and record the answers. But a typical problem develops during this period. Facilitators encourage participants to contribute ideas but then accept all answers without challenge regardless of how shallow or unthoughtful.

The third phase of facilitator development is concerned with the issue of quality in seminar results. It involves a deeper understanding of the underlying intentions of MAP and a strengthening of practical skills for leading discussions where facilitators push for genuine insights among MAP participants. This is a phase of finesse and sensitivity and is a difficult one to realise.

MAP training activities are designed to correspond to these three stages: 1) an orientation period, 2) "on-the-job training" in the field, and 3) advanced MAP facilitator training.

MAP Orientation

The purpose of the MAP orientation is to introduce prospective facilitators to a whole new approach to the learning process. Traditional roles are turned upside-down in MAP so that participants are considered "experts" rather than uninformed students. MAP utilises sophisticated techniques for enabling groups to draw upon their own latent knowledge. Though some national programmes have attempted to demonstrate MAP techniques in a classroom

setting, it is more effective to introduce future facilitators to MAP techniques
through a week-long orientation seminar that includes observation of an
actual MAP seminar in the field. An orientation seminar often appears as
follows.

Monday:	introduction to the national design of CMPP
Tuesday:	observation of the first day of a CMPP Seminar in a primary cooperative society
Wednesday:	observation of the second day of a CMPP Seminar in the primary society
Thursday:	half-day visit to another society to see the results of CMPP after the completion of a seminar; reflections on the field trips
Friday:	introduction to the "Facilitators Guide" and review of future schedules for "on-the-job training"

It is important in the orientation seminar to have all participants in
residence together at the training venue for logistical reasons, especially
transport. This includes those who live nearby and who might want to stay
at home. Distractions away from the seminar hamper their participation.
Such non-residential participants often arrive very late for the daily sessions.
This is always a problem, but for a seminar that involves extensive field trips,
it is disastrous.

On-the-Job Training

After becoming familiar with the participatory approach of CMPP by
observing seminars in the field, novice facilitators begin developing their
skills by actually standing before groups and leading workshops. For this
experience to be most effective, new facilitators need to lead these seminars
while being observed and critiqued by master facilitators. A helpful work-
sheet for appraising CMPP facilitators during "on-the-job" training is easily
adapted from work by Community Organisation Consultants in Nairobi
(Damen).

The number of seminars for effective "on the job training" is indefinite.
The more, however, the better. Initially, novice facilitators are preoccupied
with their own performance. They are primarily concerned with doing the
right thing at the right time. Most novice facilitators must lead workshops in
seminars for at least four or five times before they become familiar enough
with the process to redirect their attention away from what they are doing to
what participants are really saying and experiencing. "On-the-job training"
should, therefore, last long enough for facilitators to be involved in at least
half a dozen CMPP seminars.

A small number of experienced facilitators is a major constraint to the rapid expansion of a programme through "on-the-job training." But if a national programme is ultimately to be an effective one, this step in the training process cannot be rushed.

Advanced Facilitator Training

After novice facilitators have gained some practical experience through "on-the-job training," they are ready to sharpen their skills and deepen their understanding about the CMPP approach. Though topics of advanced training can be introduced at an earlier stage, it is done so with limited results. It is difficult for novice facilitators to fully grasp insights of advanced facilitation until they have gained a breadth of experience with which to refer. For an advanced facilitators training seminar to be effective, it must involve a significant commitment of time. National CMPP programmes have found that two full weeks are usually required.

Some topics and activities typically included in an advanced CMPP facilitators training seminar are:

- up-dating of current CMPP activities in the districts and provinces
- extensive examination of underlying theoretical assumptions of the participatory approach of CMPP
- numerous exercises for becoming more familiar with these theoretical foundations
- study from other sources on the role of "animators"
- development of techniques for ensuring high levels of active participation by seminar participants, especially by those less inclined to contribute their ideas in a public forum, e.g. women, less prosperous farmers, etc.
- development of techniques for ensuring high quality of thinking when participants create CMPP plans
- considerations about members education concerning the rights and obligations of co-op members prior to CMPP seminars
- collection of useful baseline data at the beginning of the CMPP cycle
- adjustments to seminar procedures for holding more powerful seminars
- reflections upon the project design for CMPP in Zambia for maximum effectiveness
- testing the lessons gained in the training seminar by having facilitators conduct an actual two-day CMPP Seminar in a society
- extensive reflections on the necessary monitoring activities which are required to sustain grassroots initiatives catalysed by CMPP

review of up-coming CMPP activities and confirmation of all logistical arrangements for the following months.

In order for this type of advanced facilitators training seminar to be most effective, it needs to be held at a venue away from the everyday business of most of the facilitators. It is important that participants in this seminar devote their attention to the training seminar. Residential living at the site of the training is preferable to people commuting from their homes and offices.

The training of CMPP facilitators takes place over an extended period of time. In a sense, there is no end to becoming a facilitator because it is a continual learning process. The structure of formal training in this process includes a mix of background theory and experimentation with practical techniques for leading CMPP seminars.

High Levels of Participant Involvement

In carrying out the MAP adaptations, facilitators can utilise many techniques for encouraging high levels of participation. These are systematised in the CMPP facilitator's guide, or manual.

The guide provides a blueprint of procedural steps for doing CMPP seminars. Yet good facilitators need a very clear understanding about WHY they ask the questions they do and LISTEN to the answers they receive from the participants. Stale questions parroted mindlessly from a "blueprint" will not realise the aims of CMPP. Neither will short-cuts.

The facilitator's guide is presented and elaborated upon extensively during orientation training seminars for new CMPP facilitators. Yet the challenge of training new facilitators in participatory techniques is a big one. "On-the-job" training evaluations are often the first time that many of the procedural steps of the facilitators guide are truly grasped by new facilitators. This is readily illustrated by some examples taken from monitoring visits of CMPP made by staff of the MAP project.

During the team discussion in one CMPP seminar, the facilitator gave up all responsibility for facilitating the team by naming a "team chairman" who led the discussion. This resulted in very long speeches by a very small number of vocal participants while the vast majority of other people in the team merely sat and listened. The facilitator likewise sat in silence while the team went through a very chaotic, aimless conversation. The facilitator mistakenly thought this abdication of responsibility was treating participants as "experts."

In the discussions of another workshop, participants were asked to propose self-help projects. One person in the team made a suggestion and the facilitator immediately asked if the group agreed. They said they did, so the suggestion was listed as one of their projects even though no discussion had taken place concerning its merits or feasibility.

When a second project was proposed, the facilitator immediately offered strong support for the idea by making a long speech on how the project could be implemented through a bank loan. After listening to this long speech, one person in the team simply said "we support your idea," at which time the facilitator wrote the proposed project on large paper for the plenary presentation. With that the team discussion came to an end. Only two ideas were proposed and virtually no discussion had taken place by the participants. Short-cuts to procedures described in the facilitator's guide undermined the intent of the seminar.

These problems could have been avoided had some basic guidelines in the facilitator's guide been followed. Reflecting on their "mistakes" during an "on the job training" evaluation finally allowed the new facilitators to appreciate the value of these guidelines and further expand upon them (see Appendix 2).

Because participants in many seminars are not given time to do an individual brainstorm before sharing ideas, conversations sometimes degenerate into a stale repetitious series of comments, "I support the previous idea." In one "on-the-job" evaluation, it was said that if a facilitator had stopped to ask participants to explain the "previous idea," they would probably have been unable to do so.

To avoid falling into this trap, the facilitator's guide calls for each workshop to start with a proper introduction. First, the facilitator explains that time will be given for the group to think in silence to brainstorm their own ideas as individuals. Second, the facilitator says that it is important that everyone voice their idea even if it has already been stated: simply saying that their idea has already been shared without stating it is unacceptable. Third, the facilitator urges participants not to change their mind about what to say on the basis of what others before them contributed because it is important to know what everyone thinks.

Training facilitators in techniques like these is very detailed and is very time-consuming. Classroom orientation is necessary, but such lessons are usually learned best "on the job" through the careful review and evaluation of performances by facilitators.

High-quality Thinking by Participants

In December 1990, an advanced facilitator training seminar took place in the Coast Region of Tanzania. It brought together CMPP facilitators from Kenya, Tanzania, and Zambia. The training included a demonstration CMPP seminar and follow-up meeting with two co-op societies which provided an opportunity for reflection on issues of quality.

Criticism was made about abstract obstacle statements observed in the demonstration seminar. Kenyan facilitators said they consider statements beginning with "lack of..." to be symptomatic of shallow thinking. What is the tangible, concrete manifestation of a problem alluded to by "lack of unity?" Abstract statements like "poor leadership" always have tangible manifestations, e.g. "the management committee acts in secret and does not call us to meetings to report on its activities."

The self-evaluation conversations concluded that facilitators need persistently to push groups to deeper thinking. The key, of course, to having participants name clear obstacles is for facilitators themselves to be able to distinguish the difference between "abstract" and "tangible" statements. Merely asking a lot of different questions is insufficient if facilitators cannot themselves distinguish tangible obstacles from abstract ones.

One occurrence in the demonstration follow-up meeting served as a reminder of the delicate responsibility a facilitator has for enabling participants to plan good, realistic projects. A youth group reported that they had started a carpentry project and that they had been able to make progress by borrowing some tools from within the village. A facilitator then made a strong speech about the availability of a "revolving loan fund" for obtaining tools in industrial projects. When the youth went back to their team to plan the next steps for their carpentry work, they decided to pursue a loan from this revolving fund.

It was only much later as the follow-up meeting came to an end that a villager asked a question about requirements for qualifying for a loan from the fund. It immediately became obvious that the youth did not qualify, yet their entire plan was to seek the loan. In a sense, the youth had been misled because they thought it would be a simple matter for them to obtain the loan. The common sense question which revealed the complexity involved needed to have been asked when the youth first began to consider the loan. It is the responsibility of a facilitator to ask such questions early and to steer the discussion in a different direction if the prospects are clearly deemed to be unrealistic.

When a piece of information like that of the "revolving loan fund" is shared in a CMPP seminar, it is almost always perceived by villagers to be a strong recommendation—coming from an authority figure—about what they "ought" to do. Facilitators need to be extremely careful in what they say during seminars. If facilitators are to avoid misleading participants, they must communicate, if not overstate, the difficulties involved when sharing any information about "opportunities." Better yet, proposals for future action should primarily be left to the participants themselves to make on their own. Participants do not need a lot of partial information, even when given with the best of intentions, coming from outsiders who will be uninvolved in project implementation.

Facilitators in another advanced training seminar tackled a problem that had been undermining their work. When asked to name key implementation steps, participants were often listing vague empty items like "form a committee, make a plan, follow through on committee plans." The facilitators decided to create an implementation work-sheet for participants to complete during the workshop discussions. The work-sheet has helped avoid frivolous implementation steps creeping into CMPP plans by focusing attention on practical issues of scheduling activities, gathering materials, and organising work.

Ensuring quality in CMPP planning is the most difficult skill for novice facilitators to learn and the most difficult skill for a master facilitator to teach. The examples above provide a few illustrations of how that training has occurred at various times in the context of actual field work.

Facilitator Flexibility in Follow-up Work

Because CMPP is an open-ended process, CMPP facilitators are constantly confronting unanticipated situations. Facilitators are required to respond to a host of surprises when conducting follow-up monitoring visits for CMPP. Unexpected problems are always lurking. Facilitators in the Coast Region of Tanzania confronted such a problem. The following is a brief case study that illustrates the complexity of training facilitators to do their job.

The potential involvement of other government extension officers in CMPP activities was discussed during an advanced facilitators training seminar. Unsurprisingly, any of the objectives that CMPP facilitators are trying to catalyse are ones they share with many different extension officers: community development officers are trying to encourage self-help; cooperative extension officers are trying to encourage better management of co-op societies; agricultural extension officers are trying to encourage modern practices in agriculture. These are the very types of activities that participants often plan in the CMPP seminars. Extension services are intended to provide a basic human infrastructure of expertise and support to the rural population. It is only logical, therefore, to try to bring extension officers and local people together as project-planning takes place during CMPP seminars. Accordingly, extension officers are invited to attend all CMPP seminars and are one of the most important audiences for the "Leadership Seminars" that subsequently follow.

"Self-evaluation" discussions in the Coast Region revealed that CMPP facilitators were encountering several problems in working with extension officers. Though extension officers usually appreciate the results that come from the CMPP seminars, most do not seem to understand that by building on the emergent excitement and interest catalysed by CMPP they can actually enhance their own work. Since "follow-up to self-help projects planned during CMPP seminars" does not specifically appear in their job descriptions (even though something like "encouragement of self-reliance within villages and general support of local initiatives" undoubtedly does), they seldom bother with local activities planned in CMPP seminars.

This kind of passive involvement of extension officers with CMPP activities is the norm in Tanzania. In one ward, however, there was a spectacular example of one extension officer interpreting CMPP as a threatening competitor instead of a helpful complement. Her involvement was not passive; it became actively hostile.

The circumstances of this particular situation are both interesting and informative. During a CMPP seminar, the youth planned to make and sell charcoal as an income project. As usual, the community development officer was present at this CMPP seminar when the project was planned. Once the youth began to implement their project, they decided they needed a simple shed to store their charcoal and protect it from the rain. They did not have money, however, for purchasing materials. When they discussed this problem with the community development officer, she put them in touch with a Canadian NGO (CUSO) which was operating in the area. This NGO in turn agreed to provide a small capital grant so that the youth could purchase their materials.

Though CMPP never provides this type of external support to self-help projects, it is quite happy to see people go out and promote assistance elsewhere. One could say that this extension officer's involvement with the youth after the seminar was a great example of what CMPP would like to see happen. The problem came when the CMPP facilitators returned to do the scheduled "follow-up" meeting three months later.

The youth told the facilitators that they could not attend the follow-up meeting because the community development officer insisted that they were no longer a "CMPP project" but were now a "CUSO project!" It seems that this was an important distinction to her because she was receiving "incentives" from CUSO (a bicycle and a small daily allowance to visit villages) and she wanted to show them some results of her work.

Understandably, this infuriated the CMPP facilitators. The essential issue was project identification. Charcoal-making and selling was, of course, neither a "CMPP project" nor a "CUSO project" nor a "community development officer project." Charcoal-making was the **youth's project**. CMPP, CUSO, and the community development officer merely played supporting roles. CMPP provided a structured process whereby the youth conceived of their project, planned how to do it, and reflected upon their progress in the follow-up meeting; CUSO provided important capital input. the extension officer became an enabling linkage with CUSO. These are complementary roles. The problem arose because people placed too much importance on their own particular role and forgot that the object of all their effort was to enable the youth.

There is an old saying about working together: "we can accomplish anything as long as we don't worry about who receives the credit." The facilitators were quite correct in solving the problem of the youth's hesitation to attend the follow-up meeting through the mediation of the village chairman. That, however, was only an immediate solution to the particular problem at hand. The CMPP facilitators continue to search for practical ways of working effectively with extension officers as a complement of supporting agents.

In responding to unexpected problems in monitoring and follow-up, facilitators need to have a firm understanding of their purpose and aim in doing CMPP. Because such problems are unpredictable, formal training cannot directly prepare facilitators to confront such unknown challenges. CMPP training can only set the context. The effectiveness of the training is now put to the test, for it is facilitators themselves who must then draw upon their critical intelligence and sensitivity to observe, judge, weigh up, decide, and act when confronted by unexpected and uncomfortable complications.

In such moments, the trainer can only hope that the overarching message of the training is remembered: in its essence, CMPP is only about enabling local people to be agents of their own development.

Chapter 10

SUMMARY AND CONCLUSIONS
FROM MAP FIELD WORK

This chapter is a summary of the MAP project and is divided into four sections. It begins with a brief review of the field settings where MAP was employed and is followed in the second section with a discussion about the strategic design of participatory programmes. Section three reviews insights about monitoring and evaluating participation. The final section focuses on the training of facilitators.

Field Laboratories for MAP Research

These methodologies have been put to the test in five different settings over the past three years.

MAP worked with the **Cooperative Members' Participation Programme**, CMPP, in Kenya, Tanzania, and Zambia. Though these national programmes are broadly related, the practical implementation of each has been a unique undertaking in all three countries. The basic intent of CMPP is the empowerment of ordinary members in the affairs of local co-ops, i.e. the "primary cooperative societies." During the life of the MAP project, the three national CMPPs were working in over 50 local cooperatives. Direct field activities of the MAP project with CMPP included:

- 3 CMPP Design Consultations in Tanzania
- 1 CMPP Design Consultation in Zambia
- 3 Facilitator Orientation Seminars in Zambia
- 5 Field Monitoring and Staff Self-Evaluation Exercises in Tanzania
- 1 Field Monitoring Exercise in Zambia
- 3 Advanced Facilitator Training Seminars in Tanzania
- 1 Advanced Facilitator Training Seminar in Zambia
- 4 External Evaluations in Tanzania
- 2 External Evaluations in Zambia
- 1 External Evaluation in Kenya
- 1 Regional Symposium with facilitators from all three countries.

The **Babati District Land Management Programme** in Tanzania, LAMP, was another setting for experimenting with MAP methods. The basic aim of the programme is to improve land-husbandry practices across the district. As stated in its project document, "the activities and projects in LAMP should be planned and implemented within the district by the people themselves and their organisations." Participation in environmental issues has thus been a major aspiration of the programme since its inception.

The MAP Project worked with LAMP during two phases. First, MAP assisted in designing and implementing participatory planning seminars in four pilot villages in August 1989. Second, it assisted LAMP in designing and implementing five district seminars with particular interest groups in February and March 1991. The purpose of this second type of seminar was to include the perspectives of five "constituencies" (i.e. pastoralists, small farmers, large commercial farmers, non-governmental organisations, and district administrators and elected officials) in the planning of district-wide environmental projects.

The **Integrated Rural Development Programme** in the Eastern Province of Zambia, IRDP/EP, has provided another field laboratory for testing MAP. The immediate predecessor of IRDP/EP was introduced in 1972 as part of the Swedish "Agricultural Sector Support Programme." In 1979 the name was changed to IRDP/EP to reflect its wider inclusion of more communities across the province. A third phase was introduced in 1986 when services were extended to rural communities through a decentralisation process to the District Councils. The IRDP/EP is now scheduled to come to an end in 1993 and is actively engaged in a "phasing out" programme between now and then.

MAP began its relationship with IRDP/EP in October 1989 with initial discussions about future collaboration. This set the stage for a series of "Branch Development Seminars" that eventually took place in the Chama District. The MAP Project was then involved in subsequent follow-up activities with the Chama work including an extensive evaluation in June 1991. Beyond the work in Chama, MAP assisted IRDP/EP in creating a programme design for a series of seminars to form local "Project Maintenance Committees."

In addition to these five field laboratories, the MAP Project organised three **"Participation Forums"** that brought together practitioners and academics to share insights about current trends in participatory development. Two of these were national events, one in Tanzania and one in Zambia, while the third was a regional event with delegates from Zimbabwe, Kenya, Malawi, and Zambia. The MAP Project also facilitated a major conference on members participation for the International Cooperative Alliance that involved delegates from nine Asian countries.

Strategic Design of MAP Methodology

MAP methodologies are extremely flexible. They can be utilised in almost any situation that calls for increasing the involvement of rural people. This has been amply demonstrated in the programmes that have adapted MAP methods during the past three years.

In conducting its practical research, the MAP Project has had to contend with a number of specific constraints. And as every practitioner knows, the political realities of working with actual development projects often limit the scope of available options. This is obviously true in designing of participation activities.

Though it is an immensely flexible methodology, MAP is built on specific values. These form a basic framework for discussing the strategic design of any adaptation of MAP. Many of these values are introduced as underlying assumptions of MAP in the Final Report. Three of them are especially important when considering possible choices in designing a strategy for promoting participation:

1)   - rural people can be agents of their own development;

2)   - a major change in individual self-perceptions, from passive victims to active players, is needed in many rural situations for this to occur; and

3)   - the practical experience of successfully managing small projects is a key ingredient to altering negative self-perceptions and developing self-confidence among villagers.

From the perspective held in these three points, the MAP Project has gleaned a number of strategic insights about designing participation promotion programmes.

Grassroots Mobilisation

The three values above are most easily addressed in programmes that are community-based and open-ended in regards to the planning of local projects. Such programme are particularly effective in allowing the poor to take an active role in organised efforts of rural development.

Strategic designs of MAP adaptation used in this context have enabled the formation of informal groups based on local priorities and mutual trust among peers. When local projects are planned in an open-ended way, a sense of project ownership by participants is inherent with the process. Nothing is imposed from outside.

CMPP in Tanzania has been an example of this type of approach. Though planning seminars are organised under the auspices of the primary society, projects are planned by informal groups of youth, women, and men, rather than the formal structure of the co-op. Many of the participants in these seminars are not even members of the cooperative. The long-term intention of this approach is to establish a pattern of successfully managed self-help projects: as villagers become more confident in their capacity to initiate and manage development activities, the greater the potential for local control of cooperative institutions.

Institutional Strengthening of Local Organisations

MAP methodologies can also play a creative role in strengthening local institutions. Because those who have a direct interest in an organisation are more informed and involved, participatory planning renders a greater ability to implement plans and policy. It builds teamwork and cooperation because a common context for decision-making, communication, and problem-solving is created. Participatory planning also encourages initiative and responsibility because people feel a greater sense of commitment through the ownership of a plan.

Improving the operating performance of local organisations is a strategic application of MAP methodology. CMPP in Kenya has moved steadily in the direction of strengthening primary cooperative societies and away from a strategy of involving grassroots members since it was first initiated in 1986. Though the final outcome is still uncertain, the Ministry of Cooperative Development has strongly suggested that CMPP in the future should be a programme used exclusively with elected officials of cooperative management committees.

It is important not to confuse "strengthening local organisations" with that of "grassroots mobilisation." Both are legitimate strategies for rural development and are often related but they are not synonymous. When a participation programme is designed, careful consideration needs to be given to the difference in the light of its basic objectives. Rhetoric found in many programme documents is concerned with the "poorest of the poor" but activities are focussed on leaders of local organisations. Working through established leaders is usually a very indirect way to reach marginalised members of a community.

Limited Effectiveness of External Inputs

An attitude of dependence is often a big obstacle to rural people becoming agents of their own development. The premature introduction of financial or material resources in support of local projects can be a hindrance to altering passive self-perceptions.

The MAP Project came across many examples of frustrated development projects which illustrate this point. Water-wells dug by the IRDP/EP fell into disuse when repairs were needed because local residents were waiting for the project sponsors to come back and do the job. Communal work-days in constructing a local dispensary in one Tanzanian village promptly stopped when an expatriate technician sought to support the local initiative by promising to provide metal roofing material: villagers shifted their efforts from constructing their own building to soliciting additional support from their new found-patron.

MAP, with its interest in altering self-perceptions and promoting local initiative, works best when no external resources are provided to assist people in the projects they plan. The basic message of self-reliant development thus remains simple and consistent.

Objectives of many programmes, however, often include the introduction of external support. Experiences with MAP adaptations have shown that it is possible to succeed in promoting self-reliance if resources are provided with thoughtful prudence. This was the case in the Tanzanian village of Managhat as villagers spent over a year preparing to receive grade cattle from an international donor. Planting small pastures and attending simple training sessions on the care of grade cattle were both required by the donor. These were important steps for encouraging self-reliance even as villagers anticipated the arrival of gift cows.

Since self-reliance is often seen as a key to long-term sustainability, careful thought should be given to the contradictions implied with the provision of inputs. As with other variables in the design of a programme, the question of whether to provide external resources or not needs to be answered in accordance with its fundamental objectives.

Enhancement of Women's Participation

The need to integrate women's involvement into the mainstream of rural development is increasingly recognised as a major priority in many programmes. Two approaches for ensuring women's integration were found to be helpful in conducting programmes with MAP methodology.

It was important to establish a quorum for women's attendance in MAP seminars. In the early days of the CMPP, involvement of women was always strongly encouraged. The number of women who then actually attended the planning seminars, however, was often quite small. This recurring problem finally led CMPP to establish minimum quotas for women's attendance. If a quorum was not reached by the time the seminar was to begin, then it was postponed. A strong message was thus delivered about the importance of women's participation.

Interestingly enough, teams of facilitators seldom experienced the need to cancel more than one seminar because of poor women's attendance. It may well be that through the act of cancelling, facilitators reinforced their own resolve about the seriousness of women's participation and were, therefore, able to adequately communicate this fact in subsequent visits with local leaders.

The division of men and women into separate groups during portions of a seminar also proved to be effective. Because traditional culture often subordinates female involvement, this gave women an opportunity to organise their thoughts, prepare their presentations, and sharpen their questions prior to meeting again with the men. Dividing into men's and women's teams became a means for ensuring the integration of women's insights into the deliberations of the entire community.

Follow-up Support by Facilitators

The programmes that experimented with MAP generally followed an "expansive" strategy. They were designed to reach a relatively large number of communities rather than provide intensive support to a very few. By design, facilitators in these programmes had limited opportunity to offer continued back-up support to participants. This usually consisted of follow-up meetings and monitoring visits to review progress and discuss problems concerning project implementation.

CMPP, IRDP/EP, and LAMP all largely avoided having facilitators play an intermediary role to link communities with external services and resources. The reason for this was the same as that for limiting external inputs: facilitators want to encourage self-reliance. The more that facilitators do for people, the greater the risk of developing an unintended sense of dependency.

The major challenge of a participation programme is to discern the minimum level of facilitator support that still allows the programme to be an effective catalyst for self-reliant development. A systematic pattern of monitoring visits can accomplish this. Many facilitators, however, are tempted to skimp on follow-up work so that they can conduct new seminars in additional communities; this must be strongly resisted.

Participation in Large Sectoral Programmes

MAP adaptations with programmes that are "sector specific" (e.g. health, environment, irrigation, forestry, etc.) encounter more problems in mobilising grassroots action than those that are completely open-ended. Sectoral concerns involve an element of salesmanship as local participants are asked to focus their attention on the particular interest of the outside agency. MAP is most effectively used in sectoral programmes when local people are free to decide their own responses to a designated topic. It is obvious that the more directed a programme is in its desired results, the more difficult it will be to establish a sense of local ownership for the project.

The formation of maintenance committees around projects previously funded by the IRDP/EP is an example of this type of MAP adaptation. In these planning events, the subject of discussion was determined by the existing project. The response of the community, however, was never imposed. People themselves decided how, indeed if, they would maintain the project infrastructure under consideration. The village seminars in the Babati LAMP similarly resulted in people planning their own projects.

MAP can also be beneficial to sectoral programmes with a large geographic focus. Participation helps to ensure that future proposals are sensitive to locally felt needs while the inclusion of indigenous knowledge in the planning of major projects can improve their eventual effectiveness.

The "constituency" seminars sought to have contenaing interest groups contribute their perspectives to the formation of district environmental projects; this proved to be successful. Participants also left the seminars better informed about LAMP activities. But it was difficult for participants to assume practical responsibility for their proposals.

As with the distinction between institutional strengthening and grassroots mobilisation, it is important not to confuse participation in large sectoral projects with something it is not. Such adaptations of MAP have their genuine value, but large projects are limited in their capacity to empower local people.

Monitoring and Evaluating Participation Promotion

The MAP Project has reached a number of conclusions about the monitoring and evaluation of participation promotion programmes. These are based on eight external evaluations conducted with MAP-related programmes and on the MAP Project's own extensive field work in monitoring results from two village seminars in Babati.

Qualitative Research Methods Are Essential

A combination of qualitative and quantitative methods are needed in evaluating participation. Due to the "process" nature of participation, as opposed to that of a "project" with predetermined objectives, qualitative methods are indispensable for interpreting the results of participation programmes. Qualitative methods can help avoid creating an evaluation report of isolated, unrelated, and out of context parts.

An example from one of the external evaluations of CMPP illustrates the point. The evaluators concluded that a local co-op which "only managed to buy a hammer mill" among its planned projects should be rated lower than other co-ops that completed three or four projects. Yet this simple quantitative comparison leaves many unanswered questions.

What was involved in the purchase of the hammer mill? What resources were used to buy it? From where did the resources come? What problems had to be overcome? The purchase of a hammer mill is an extremely big task for most villages. A project of that magnitude might easily explain inattention to other projects. If, on the other hand, an external source provided a very soft loan to buy the mill, then the significance of the purchase would be viewed in an entirely different light. The holistic approach of qualitative methods can enable an evaluator's understanding about the complex issues involved in participatory processes.

Understanding the Participatory Process Requires Familiarity

Evaluating participation is best conducted when an evaluator has several occasions to monitor activities over an extended period of time. A "snapshot" approach of collecting information at a single moment severely limits an evaluator's understanding of the evolutionary process of participation. The ability to follow developments over time was essential in the MAP Project's evaluation work in the two Babati villages.

Sorting out complicated interdependent variables requires a high degree of familiarity between the evaluator and the subjects of the evaluation. This is usually shunned in traditional evaluations because of the perceived need to preserve a sense of objectivity. Qualitative evaluation, however, requires the active involvement and commitment of the evaluator as subtle changes evolve during participation activities. This discourages the detachment and distance that are often characteristics of other evaluation approaches.

Evaluating Participation Is Not the Same as "Participatory Evaluation"

"Participatory evaluation" may well be a part of an evaluation, indeed it would be a gross contradiction not to include it given the general bottom-up nature of participation promotion, but participatory evaluation is not a substitute for evaluation per se. The two have different aims. Participatory evaluation is a learning technique for improving project implementation. The evaluation of participation, however, seeks to understand and interpret a delicate development process. The former asks "how can we be more effective in our work?" while the latter asks "what impact has occurred?"

Training of Facilitators

MAP training activities have been organised in three phases: 1) an orientation period, 2) "on-the-job training" in the field, and 3) advanced facilitator training.

Facilitator Orientation Happens Best in the Field

The purpose of the MAP orientation is to introduce prospective facilitators to a whole new approach to the learning process. Traditional roles are turned upside down as participants are treated as "experts" rather than uninformed students. While some programmes have introduced MAP techniques in a classroom setting, these are difficult concepts to teach in the abstract. It is far more effective to introduce future facilitators to techniques of participation by having them observe an actual MAP seminar in the field and then reflect upon the experience. Novice facilitators thereby become better acquainted with the intent, format, and logistics of the programme.

Facilitators Learn Best through On-the-Job Training

After becoming familiar with the participatory approach of MAP by observing seminars, novice facilitators begin developing their skills by actually standing before groups and leading workshops. New facilitators lead these seminars while being closely observed and critiqued by master facilitators.

Though the number of seminars for effective on-the-job training is indefinite, the more the better. Initially, novice facilitators are preoccupied with their own performance and are primarily concerned with doing the right thing at the right time. Most novice facilitators lead workshops four or five times before they become familiar enough with the process to redirect their attention away from what they themselves are doing to what participants are really saying and experiencing. On-the-job training should, therefore, last long enough for facilitators to be involved in at least half a dozen MAP seminars.

A small number of experienced facilitators to oversee on-the-job training is a major constraint to the rapid expansion of a programme, but if a programme is ultimately to be an effective one, this step in the training cannot be rushed.

Advanced Training Events Are a Key to Sustaining Performance

The third phase of a facilitator's development is concerned with issues of quality. It involves a deeper understanding about the underlying intentions of MAP and a strengthening of practical skills so facilitators can enable participants to dig deeper for genuine insights.

Topics of advanced training include an extensive examination of theoretical assumptions of the participatory methods; the introduction and practice of techniques for ensuring high levels of active participation by all seminar participants, especially women and less prosperous farmers; the introduction and practice of techniques for ensuring high-quality thinking during each step of the planning process. Premature introduction of these topics before facilitators have gained a breadth of experience with which to refer is usually a waste of time.

Facilitation skills emerge from the experience of leading seminars and careful reflection on the results. In this way, through a lot of hard work, facilitators move toward fulfilling their responsibilities of empowering villagers to play an active role in rural development.

Conclusion

The methodologies developed by the MAP Project have been carefully tested in numerous programme settings in Kenya, Tanzania, and Zambia. This has resulted in a wealth of practical insights concerning the strategic design of programmes, the training of facilitators, and the evaluation of participation promotion. Field manuals have been prepared from these experiences so that MAP can be easily adapted to other development programmes in the future.

PART TWO: THE MAP FACILITATOR'S HANDBOOK

Chapter 11

METHODS FOR ACTIVE PARTICIPATION

Part Two of this volume serves as a handbook for facilitators who are responsible for promoting rural participation in the field. This chapter is a restatement about MAP and the role of a facilitator for introducing the techniques and methods described in the handbook.

MAP, Rural People, and Development

Participation promotion is about change. Many rural people, especially women and those of low economic standing, have been forgotten and ignored in organised development activities. Development professionals often refer to these and other factors as "marginalisation." By whatever name, it has left many scars among rural people: the prevalence of passivity and fatalism, a firm belief that their opinions and thoughts can be of little influence in affecting development efforts, illusionary expectations of donors and officials.

Many people in rural areas have become accustomed to waiting for outsiders to do something on their behalf. Repeatedly rural people have been informed through the actions of officials, if not through their formal speeches, that development affairs should be left to outside experts. It is not surprising, therefore, that villagers often begin to see themselves as **passive objects** of development projects rather than active players in the development process.

Passive attitudes are rooted in self-perceptions that have grown over a lifetime of reinforcing messages. The "images" that people have of themselves determine the way they think and act. Correspondingly, when a significant change in a person's behaviour occurs, the change can be traced to a shift in self-images.

Villagers often see themselves as passive objects rather than as active players.

MAP aggressively challenges the passive attitudes found in rural situations and aims to convey one central message in all that it does: rural people can be agents of their own development! There is no need for villagers to wait for others to take charge of development activities, be they government officials, academic experts, or foreign donors.

MAP methodology follows a simple premise in its approach: attitudes and self-perceptions are more effectively addressed and potentially altered when people EXPERIENCE a new reality rather than when they are TOLD that they ought to think and act differently. The basic means for enabling this to happen in MAP are the conducting of participatory planning seminars followed by the successful implementation of self-help projects.

With MAP, **participants are treated as experts**, i.e. as people who have a wealth of latent knowledge gained through years of practical experience. The opinions and ideas of villagers are both solicited and honoured as participants are guided through a structured process to dig insights out of their accumulated wisdom. As self-help projects are planned using MAP techniques, villagers often realise through their own interaction with each other that many of their suggestions are over-ambitious and cannot be realised.

Women's participation is a high priority in MAP methodology and the target for women's involvement is often as high as 50 per cent. If quorums for women's attendance are not met, programmes using MAP often postpone or cancel planning events. When such a cancellation occurs, a strong message is communicated about the importance of women's participation.

MAP provides a **forum for farmers** to freely express their concerns, to ask their questions, make their demands, and state their desires. There are usually few opportunities in rural areas where local leaders must face ordinary members of the community in an open-ended "question time." The content of discussions is never predefined in MAP activities. All suggestions and opinions are considered, thereby allowing all social strata within a community to advocate their interests.

Though MAP can be used in many differing situations, it works best when **no external inputs** are provided to assist people in projects they plan. There are, of course, limitations on what very poor villagers can do solely on the basis of their own resources; people can only lift themselves so far by pulling on their "bootstraps." But a shift in self-perception, from a passive victim to an active player, is a realistic expectation of self-help activities. Conversely, the premature introduction of external capital from a charitable patron sends the wrong message. It undermines self-confidence and reinforces a passive attitude by communicating that it does indeed pay to wait.

Premature introduction of resources can reinforce passive attitudes.

The projects planned in MAP workshops are small self-help projects that people can accomplish by themselves without depending on outside resources. Through the implementation of small-scale projects villagers can gain simple experience in the **practical management** of organisational details like budgeting time, working together, and accounting for funds. Important organisational skills can develop slowly but substantially on a solid foundation of local project implementation. Small successes breed confidence for bigger undertakings.

Participation and Project Ownership

Participation promotion programmes vary considerably in approach and design. Most aim in one form or another to enhance a sense of local ownership in development projects. Some mobilise villagers in open-ended projects where activities are based entirely upon local perceptions of felt needs. Others seek to establish integrating partnerships into larger development schemes to address specific objectives.

MAP methodologies are applicable in most participation programmes because they focus on involving people in the process of planning and implementing projects, a process often referred to as a "project cycle." Typically this includes problem identification, project planning, implementation, and evaluation.

This cycle is systematized in MAP by a sequence of steps. In each step, local villagers take centre stage and are the primary actors as they plan and implement project activities. Facilitators play a supporting role by enabling active participation and ensuring quality thinking.

The MAP process begins with the "current situation" in a preparation meeting when base-line data is collected. The next steps are usually taken in a participatory "planning seminar:" the vision, obstacles, proposals, project selection, and implementation plans. "Monitoring" of the implementation phase takes place in a series of follow-up visits and meetings. Finally, a "participatory evaluation" session ends the process. Or perhaps better said, it starts the process all over again as the evaluation session reviews the new situation which has emerged from the preceding activities and new plans are made.

MAP has structured each of these steps in a series of meetings and workshops during which time rural villagers are asked to consider particular questions:

CURRENT SITUATION - what is the pertinent information that describes the present reality of the area?

PRACTICAL VISION - what realistic hopes and dreams do participants have for this community or organisation?

OBSTACLES - what is preventing the practical vision from being realised?

PROPOSALS - how can these obstacles be overcome, by-passed, or eliminated?

SELF-HELP PROJECTS - what small projects would start the journey toward realising the vision?

IMPLEMENTATION PLANS - who, what, where, when, and how shall these projects be accomplished?

MONITORING OF IMPLEMENTATION WORK - what progress has been made in implementing the projects; what difficulties are being experienced and how can they be overcome?

PARTICIPATORY EVALUATION - what has been achieved, how is the situation now different, what needs to happen next?

Answering these questions is a big and complicated task even for those who are professionally trained in the formulation of project plans. If great care is not taken, villagers can easily fall into aimless and prolonged discussions as they wrestle with these big questions. Avoiding these pitfalls is the responsibility of facilitators. They guide a participatory planning process so that quality plans can be made within a very short period of time.

The Role of Facilitators

Facilitators play an indispensable role in promoting participation. They either make or break a programme because they are the only ones in a position to make the theories of participation come alive in practice.

Being a facilitator is a new and unfamiliar role to many people. Teachers and conventional extension officers are expected to convey information on particular subjects and thereby play the role of an expert. As expert authorities, they talk about the correct way to do things. Extension officers are additionally expected, in many circumstances, to "sell" a programme or policy and to have people fall into line behind objectives planned by central bureaucracies.

In sharp contrast, facilitators do not tell anyone what to do and avoid acting like an expert. They advocate no particular programme nor persuade people to take any predetermined action. Their job is to enable rural villagers

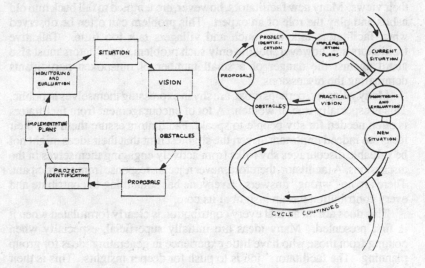

Steps in a project cycle.

to think, reflect, and act in a self-reliant manner. It often means convincing people that they have an important role to play in rural development. Facilitators enable villagers to get into the habit of trusting their own ideas and digging for deeper insights.

Becoming a MAP facilitator is an on-going learning process. No one is simply born a natural facilitator. Facilitators work as a team and learn from one another. The most valuable training they receive is "on-the-job" training. Facilitators are continually reflecting on their performance and are constantly thinking about how they might be able to improve their skills.

No MAP seminar is ever complete until facilitators debrief themselves on what took place. They review each other's performances by asking about the strengths and weaknesses of each facilitator; they discuss practical ways that each might improve during the next seminar. In order for such observations to be meaningful, of course, every facilitator will need to have been extremely attentive to all that took place during the course of the entire seminar.

Facilitators have two major overarching responsibilities entrusted to them. They enable every participant to contribute ideas to the discussions and then ensure that quality thinking has gone into the planning.

The first responsibility is to enable and encourage all participants to share their views. Many new facilitators, however, are tempted to fall back into old habits and play the role of an expert. This problem can often be observed when facilitators talk too much and villagers talk too little. Talkative facilitators are, however, not the only such problem. Facilitators must also guard against the danger of a small number of outspoken participants dominating the discussions.

Many villagers, perhaps most, are shy in expressing themselves in public. This is especially true of women. A lot of encouragement from facilitators is often needed for shy people to speak. Facilitators assure them that their ideas are indeed important. Even the slightest hint that their ideas might not be valuable discourages shy folks from actively engaging themselves in the discussions. A facilitator, therefore, never rejects a response from a participant. There are no "wrong" answers. Everyone has something to contribute and every contribution has an insight at its core.

This does not mean that every contribution is clearly formulated when it is first presented. Many ideas are initially superficial, especially when coming from those who have little experience in generating ideas for group planning. The facilitators' job is to push for deeper insights. This is their second major responsibility. Facilitators ensure quality thinking on the part of participants.

This is not easy. Since facilitators want to avoid acting like an expert, they refrain from "correcting" participants. Rather, they ask appropriate questions

No MAP seminar is complete until facilitators reflect on their skills.

that enable villagers to think more deeply for themselves. Knowing that they should not act like an expert, many new facilitators tend to neglect their responsibilities for ensuring quality thinking. They place their emphasis on encouraging people to speak and accept all answers without challenge regardless of how shallow or unthoughtful: they fear that probing questions might discourage participants from contributing ideas.

Good facilitators learn to perform a balancing act. On the one hand they treat participants as those who have a wealth of practical wisdom and encourage active participation. On the other hand, they go beneath the surface and dig deeper for true insights to ensure high-quality results.

How facilitators balance these two perspectives depends upon the unique characteristics of a group. If participants are easily contributing ideas and are not afraid to express their opinions, then more emphasis is placed upon pushing for quality thinking. If participants are shy and reluctant to share their ideas, then facilitators hold back from challenging responses in a search for deeper insights until the group gains some self-confidence.

Experienced facilitators usually follow a general rule: place more emphasis on enabling active participation during the early steps of the planning process (i.e. the vision, obstacles, and proposals) and then shift to ensuring quality thinking towards the end of the process (i.e. planning self-help projects and implementation steps). Several particular techniques can help a facilitator to maintain an effective balance between these essential responsibilities. It is to these that we now turn.

Chapter 12

TECHNIQUES FOR ENABLING BROAD PARTICIPATION

The active involvement of villagers in the planning and implementation of rural development activities is a central aim for many programmes. It is a mistake to think, however, that if rural people are merely given an opportunity to be involved then fruitful participation will automatically follow. Many **pitfalls** await the unwary facilitator when villagers come to plan: repetitious speeches, wandering discussions, dominating leaders, petty arguments, emotionally charged sidetracks, bored silence, inconclusive results.

MAP employs a number of techniques to enable participatory planning events to be productive experiences. Three basic techniques are reviewed in this chapter. The first concerns techniques of leading "discussions." The second focuses on techniques for generating and organising large amounts of information; collectively, these are known as the "workshop" method. Though conventional lecturing can often be lethal to participation, the final technique found in the chapter concerns the preparation and delivery of effective "presentations."

Discussion Techniques

One friend meets another on the way to the coffee shop and says, "I heard you went to a conference last week. How was it?" A quick response follows, "Oh, it was fine. I had a nice time." End of discussion.

Perhaps the question was casually asked, more of a greeting than a serious enquiry, and if so the quick end to the discussion was an adequate response for both parties. But often such questions are asked in the hope of starting a serious conversation. In that regard, the conversation was a disappointment.

An entirely different conversation would have occurred had a few basic questions like these been asked instead. "I heard you went to a conference last week:

(1) Where did it take place?
(2) Who were some of the other delegates?
(3) What were some of the different sessions?
(4) Which session did you find most interesting?
(5) What did you learn from the discussions?
(6) How do you plan to use any of this in your work?"

Answers to these questions would almost certainly have produced a conversation that shared genuine concerns. It would have done so because the sequence of questions followed a natural flow of the thought process. It followed a progression of questions through four levels: objective, reflective, interpretive, and decisional.

The conversation began with **objective** questions, numbers 1 through 3, that required very little thinking. These first-level questions were simple observations that comprised a little "fact-finding mission." Basic information was collected: "where did the conference take place, who was there, what was discussed?" A second-level **reflective** question was asked next, "what did you find most interesting?" With reflective questions, people begin to consider where they stand in relationship to the objective facts. This step in the sequence involves questions of emotions, feelings, or associations.

An **interpretive** question followed, "what did you learn?" At this level, people consider issues of meaning, values, or purpose. The final question asked, "how do you intend to apply insights gained from the conference," was at the **decisional** level of thought. Here, the person was asked about personal resolutions for the future.

The sequence of questions moved the conversation from surface observations to deeper considerations and responses. If the sequence had been jumbled, the natural flow of the thought process would have been broken and the conversation would have become disjointed and confusing.

A simple illustration shows the natural flow of thought through the four levels (Spencer). Imagine yourself being confronted by a group of armed thieves. You quickly note the situation: "there are two of them, they have knives, I am alone, they are asking me for my money." **Objective level**.

Next you respond emotionally: "I don't want to lose my money, I'm afraid of being hurt or killed, I don't like these people, I wish I was safe at home instead of here." **Reflective level**.

Then you interpret the situation: "I would rather lose my money than my life; these people want my money and will take it the hard way or the easy way; if I fight, I'm sure to get hurt and probably lose my money, too; if I give them my money they'll probably leave me alone." **Interpretive level**.

Finally, you decide on a course of action: "I will give them my money without resisting. As soon as they are out of sight, I'll call the police. Starting tomorrow, I'll never again carry more money than I can afford to lose and never walk alone when I do." **Decisional level.**

Leading group discussion builds on this natural thought process. The same sequence of questions is used every time while the content of questions varies according to the topic under consideration.

Examples of Group Discussion Questions

The practical uses for group discussions are countless. In participation promotion programmes, group discussions are a regular feature in formal interaction with participants. They are also useful in staff-debriefing sessions. Below are some examples of different types of discussions that might typically occur while conducting participation programmes. Each example lists some possible questions in a sequence that follows the four levels of the thought process.

Introduction discussion for a village planning event

Objective level:
> - what are some development activities that are currently taking place in this community?
> - who are some of the people who are presently involved?
> - what problems are these activities trying to solve?

Reflective level:
> - which development activities are people most pleased with?
> - when you think back to the past, what have been some of the biggest success stories for this community?

Interpretive level:
> - why were these activities so successful?
> - what lessons can be learned from those experiences that will help solve development problems in the future?

Decisional level:
> - what would be required of you if you were serious about applying those lessons again in the future?

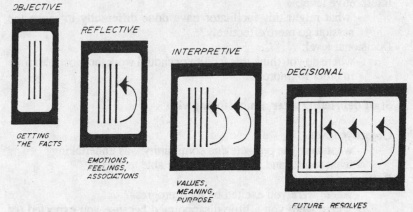

OBJECTIVE

REFLECTIVE

INTERPRETIVE

DECISIONAL

GETTING
THE FACTS

EMOTIONS,
FEELINGS,
ASSOCIATIONS

VALUES,
MEANING,
PURPOSE

FUTURE RESOLVES

Facilitators keep a balance between encouraging villagers to participate as local experts and pushing them to think deeper for greater quality in their plans.

Reflection on a proposed self-help project

Objective level:
- what problem would this project help to solve?
- what resources are necessary to do this project?

Reflective level:
- what has been the past experience of this community in trying to address this problem?
- what has prevented this problem from being solved before?

Interpretive level:
- how might these issues be overcome?
- what practical details need to be organised?
- what coordination is required?

Decisional level:
- when do you need to meet again to plan your next steps?
- who will make sure this meeting happens?

Reflection on a facilitator's performance

Objective level:
- what were some comments or phrases that you can remember this facilitator saying while leading the session?
- what were some reactions from participants that you can recall?

Reflective level:
- what did this facilitator do very well? what were some strengths?
- where did the facilitator encounter some difficulties?

Interpretive level:
>   - what might this facilitator have done differently to make the session go more effectively?

Decisional level:
>   - where do you think this facilitator should work the most next time in order to improve?

Staff debriefing after a monitoring visit

Objective level:
>   - what were the projects this community was undertaking?
>   - what results and progress were we able to see?

Reflective level:
>   - where were you excited by their progress?
>   - where were you a little disappointed because you expected (or hoped) to see more?

Interpretive level:
>   - what problems are slowing them down or are causing them to become stuck?
>   - how might they overcome these problems?

Decisional level:
>   - what can we do as facilitators to encourage these people in doing their projects?
>   - what can we do in the future to help other communities avoid these same problems when we go to work with them?

Hints for Facilitating Successful Group Discussions

Problems often arise as new facilitators lead group discussions. Below are some points of advice on how to prepare and conduct successful group discussions.

Timing

Group discussions on any one particular topic usually take place within 30 minutes or less. If more time is required, the subject is probably too large and should be broken down into smaller discussions.

Preparing good questions

Prepare for group discussions by doing a brainstorm of possible questions pertinent to the subject. Avoid questions that can be answered with a simple yes or no since they tend to end discussions rather than open them up. Take the list of potential questions and order them according to the four levels. As the questions are ordered, other questions may come to mind and these, too, can be added to the list. No level is to be omitted, so look for gaps where additional questions might need to be added.

Repetitive, vague, or tangential questions are eliminated. Once a draft of questions has been created, facilitators review every question by asking themselves "is the question clear? how might people answer it? why is it important? what am I hoping to accomplish by asking it?" Once the facilitator is satisfied with the questions, they are then reordered within each level into an easy flowing sequence.

Starting the discussion

Clearly inform group participants about the topic of the discussion and remind them of its importance. New facilitators often err by launching into a series of questions without explaining the purpose of the discussion. The first question should be particularly precise and unambiguous. Answers should be obvious so that everyone can easily respond without much thinking.

Enabling everyone to participate

Because it is important for everyone to speak at some point in a discussion, it is often a good idea to have everyone in the group answer an early question in the sequence by going from one person to the next. This quickly allows everyone in the group to become accustomed to the idea of making contributions to the discussion.

In large groups, a facilitator can have part of the group answer one question and then have other parts of the group answer a second and third. This avoids boredom with repetitious answers, keeps the thought process actively alive, and enables everyone to make a public statement.

Even when the facilitator asks open-ended questions which anyone can answer, mental notes (if not written notes) should be kept about who is answering how often. If someone has been especially quiet for a long time, the facilitator might ask a direct question: "Mrs Tembo, we haven't heard from you in a while; what do your think about this?"

Dealing with silences

It is not unusual for silences to occur with many groups, particularly if they are unaccustomed to group discussions. Be prepared to rephrase the question in several different ways. If participants seem particularly confused about a question even after it has been rephrased, a facilitator might provide an answer as an example. This often helps to clarify the question.

Keeping the discussion on course

Sometimes participants provide answers that cause the discussion to go astray. A facilitator can bring the discussion back to the subject by repeating the last question or by reviewing previous answers that remained on the subject. A facilitator can acknowledge a distracting comment while also "bracketing" it, e.g. "that is an important concern and later when we turn to that subject we will want to take it up again" and then repeat the question of the moment.

Dealing with arguments

Disagreements are not necessarily bad. A problem arises when participants tend to get stuck in the argument. It is important in strong arguments to clarify the points of disagreement and make sure that the problem is not merely one of misunderstood communication. A facilitator can either summarise the disagreement, or can ask someone else who is not directly involved to do so. Once differing points of view have been clarified, the facilitator can ask the group "do we understand each person's point of view?" To bring the debate to an end, the facilitator might say something like "as we consider this question some more, we will have to be sure to include both of these points of view in our deliberations. Now let's move on to another question."

Keeping the discussion practical

Abstract responses are often made by participants that reflect vague ideas rather than experience. Asking for an example helps to clarify the thinking of participants. For example, if someone says they hope to see "improved education in the community," a facilitator might ask "can you give us an example of what you mean by 'improved education'? how would you know if education has improved?"

Dealing with dominating participants

Some participants want to talk all the time. When someone answers questions at the expense of others, a facilitator can respond in a number of different ways. One is to simply avoid eye contact with the one who is speaking too much and, thereby, refrain from granting "recognition" to speak. If all else fails, the facilitator can politely but firmly say, "we appreciate your comments, but since you have already contributed some of your ideas, let's listen to some others before you add more."

Keeping track of the discussions

Make brief notes of comments made during the discussion. Reference can be made to these at appropriate moments, "you mentioned these ideas," and then read the list back to the group, "which are the most important?" A facilitator can also ask a member of the group to take notes. If this is done, be sure to utilise those notes in some manner. It dishonours people to ask them to do a task and then make no use of their work.

Bringing the discussion to a close

When the discussion is brought to its end, the facilitator quickly reviews some of the main points. If notes have been taken, say how they will be used. Remind participants about the purpose of the discussion and how that purpose has now been realised.

These practical hints will assist a new facilitator in leading effective discussions. The discussion technique itself is a helpful way of introducing subjects or reflecting upon work in the planning of group projects. It is very difficult, however, for firm resolutions and practical plans to emerge from general discussions. The following section presents additional techniques that enable broad participation in the planning of projects.

Three Workshop Techniques

It is a delicate task to enable many different people to participate in the collective analysis of problems and the formulation of solutions. The purpose of a "workshop" is to move from the diverse ideas and insights of many individuals towards a shared understanding about an issue under consideration. Three basic techniques make up the "workshop" methodology. The first involves a **brainstorm** of information while the second focuses on **organising data**. The third technique aims at reaching a **group consensus** through the naming of agreed upon categories.

The particularities of these techniques will vary according to the topic of specific workshops. Later, in Chapter 14, the workshop method will be reviewed in regard to different aspects of the planning process: vision, obstacles, proposals, project selection, and implementation planning. The basic principles of the workshop method, however, remain essentially the same throughout.

Workshops can take place with any size group. The larger the group, however, the more important it is to divide into smaller sub-groups, or teams, at different stages of the workshop. When groups are too large, it is difficult for everyone to contribute ideas to discussions. Smaller team discussions allow this to happen. Teams then report back in plenary sessions to the larger group.

Workshops, like discussions, begin with a clear explanation about the purpose of the exercise and the anticipated products and outcomes. The parameters of the workshop are thereby clearly established.

Disciplined Brainstorms

Brainstorms best occur in small groups that number no more than a dozen or so participants. If a group is larger than that, then it is best to divide it into teams for brainstorm work. Though brainstorming is a group exercise, it starts with the individual. The quality of any brainstorm is determined by the seriousness with which individuals do their original thinking.

The discussion method follows four levels of the thought process.

Once individuals have completed their own thinking on the subject, ideas are then shared among the participants and a collective brainstorm list is created that includes all of the ideas. Below are some practical hints and guidelines that will help a facilitator lead productive brainstorming sessions.

Clearly introduce the brainstorm topic

The topic of the brainstorm is introduced by a facilitator who seeks to ensure that it is clearly understood by everyone. Before participants start to brainstorm, the question is written on the wall and the facilitator asks if it makes sense. If there is any possibility of confusion, the facilitator might provide an example or ask for a participant to give one.

Have individuals create solitary lists

Participants are given time to think and collect their thoughts before anyone shares their ideas publicly. This is best done during a few minutes of total silence while participants list their ideas on a piece of note paper. If such materials are unavailable, or if participants are illiterate, then they can be given time to make their lists mentally. The facilitator encourages participants to write down as many ideas as possible. Every idea that comes to mind at this stage should be jotted down even if later it might be discarded. Even seemingly foolish ideas can at times spark a genuine insight on a related idea.

Set the ground rules

Before asking participants to share items from their list, the facilitator explains that everyone will be asked to contribute an idea but that there is no time for long speeches. Participants are asked to boil down their ideas before they share them. Each idea should be stated in a single sentence. Additional ideas will be received only after everyone has spoken. Setting these ground rules allows the facilitator to refer back to them with a polite reminder when they are broken.

Have every participant contribute at least one idea

Go around the group, from one person to the next, asking for the contribution of an idea. If a participant repeats an idea expressed by someone else, no problem, but everyone needs to speak. Once everyone has been called upon to speak, then the discussion can be opened to anyone who wants to make additions to the brainstorm list.

Start with someone other than a leader

Begin listing brainstorm items by asking someone other than a leader to speak first. In rural villages, leaders often sit together, so begin on the opposite side of the group. Because they are leaders, their ideas can subtly intimidate other participants from expressing their true opinions. As a general rule, it is best to have the leaders state their ideas last rather than first.

No wrong answers

The purpose of a brainstorm is to generate a lot of ideas from many different sources. It also allows participants to view ideas through each other's eyes. Do not try to weed out poor ideas while building the initial brainstorm. Since it is important that everyone understands what is being said, the most appropriate questions in brainstorm sessions are ones of clarity. If a point is confusing, facilitators ask the author of the idea to make a (very) brief explanation.

Record all ideas

Write down everyone's idea. The practical means for doing this will depend upon the materials available. The brainstorm list might be written on a blackboard or large manila sheets so everyone can see the ideas. Another technique is to write a summary of each idea on an individual sheet of paper or index card. If circumstances make it impossible for any of these, then the facilitator writes all ideas on a piece of notepaper so that they can be read back to the group when the time comes to discuss them.

Women's involvement

It is important to integrate women into the planning process. But because traditional culture has often subordinated female participation, the insights of rural women tend to become overshadowed by the dominating presence of men. A helpful technique for ensuring that women's ideas are highlighted is to have women meet in small teams by themselves. This is not "segregation" or "isolation." It is rather a practical measure to assist women in organising their thoughts and empowering their presentation so that a genuine integration of their ideas can occur once men and women are reconvened in the plenary session.

Brainstorming is the first step in the workshop method. The practical points described above will assist facilitators to lead brief but productive brainstorming sessions. The next step is to organise the information.

Organising Information

Most raw brainstorm lists are a wild, untidy hodgepodge of ideas. The bigger the group contributing to the brainstorm, the more likely is this the case. For brainstorm lists to become useful, the information needs to be organised. Involving participants in this process is the second technique of the workshop method.

Brainstorm lists are often generated in small team discussions and then reported back to the whole group in a plenary session. It is in these plenaries that facilitators have the group organise brainstorm ideas. Quite simply, this means **putting similar ideas together**. Many, if not most, of these combinations will be obvious to a group as they review the brainstorm.

Other items will be more difficult to put together. Facilitators have participants "intuit" relationships by asking them to explain ways that different ideas might fit together. Such comments often spark new insights among other participants who might see a slightly different way of combining ideas. This give and take of organising data helps to build a common understanding among participants of the topic under consideration.

There are several practical hints which can assist facilitators as brainstorms are organised by participants.

Keep brainstorm information visible

When information from a brainstorm is being organised, it is important to have all ideas placed on a wall (or easel) in front of the group so that every participant can easily read them. They might be written on a blackboard or on large manila sheets. Having brainstorm items taped to the wall on individual cards or sheets of paper is a particularly good way to display information, but logistical arrangements do not always allow for this to happen.

Make obvious combinations first

Brainstorm items are put together by similarities. A clear criterion for organising similar ideas is stated by the facilitator. For example, in a "vision" workshop, the criterion is similar "anticipated accomplishments" while in an "obstacles" workshop items are organised by "common root problems." The organising exercise begins by quickly putting together those items that obviously go together.

Don't force information together prematurely

If there is any initial hesitation or disagreement on the part of the group to put brainstorm items together, then facilitators keep them separated until later. After all items have been reviewed and obvious combinations have been made, then those items for which participants were uncertain can be discussed and included into the emerging categories.

Avoid naming the categories

The names for categories emerge from the items that are included within it. Categories are literally "redefined" every time new items are added. Giving a category a name before all of the brainstorm items have been organised can limit the category and potentially exclude possible items. Conversely, category names can also be so general that subtle differences between items tend to be overlooked all together.

A good technique for organising data is to label emerging categories with symbols like x,+,o,*, so that the categories can be referred to as "stars" or "circles" instead of words that convey actual meaning. Also avoid labelling categories with letters or numbers because they imply a ranking order. Symbols are neutral and avoid problems of premature naming.

When blackboards or large manila sheets are used for displaying lists, the same symbol can be placed next to similar brainstorm items. If index cards or small sheets of paper are used, symbols can be placed with clusters of similar cards as they are moved around on the wall.

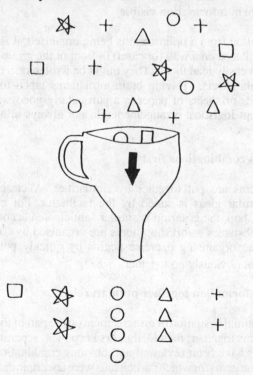

Brainstorming sessions begin by participants' individual thinking.

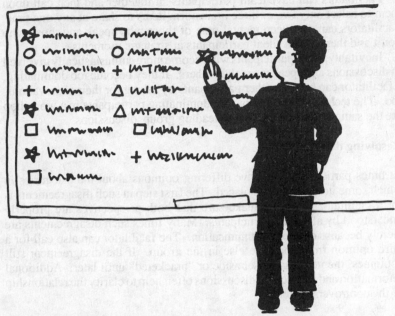

Information is organised from a brainstorm by putting similar ideas together.

Aim for a good spread of information

Categories emerge from the group discussions and it is, therefore, impossible to know exactly how many categories will finally be decided upon. However, it is helpful for a facilitator to anticipate a general range for the number of categories. The purpose of the categories is to help participants make an analysis of particular workshop topics. The anticipated range, therefore, is large enough that insights are not buried in a few generalities but not so large that the number of categories are another long list. Six to ten categories is often a good rule of thumb for most group work.

Keep the whole group involved

Organising brainstorm information into categories is an extended dialogue between a facilitator and the group. Large groups are divided into teams so that every participant can contribute to a brainstorm. When information is organised in large plenaries, however, it is often impractical to have every participant actually speak. In these circumstances, facilitators use innovative means to keep participants involved.

Facilitators can have team participants sit together and then call upon them to select only two or three brainstorm items to share at any one time. Facilitators can also keep mental note of those who speak and those who don't and then call on silent participants at strategic moments.

Inevitably, some participants will become more enthusiastically involved in discussions and speak more than others. If they become too dominating, a facilitator can bring in other participants by asking for their observations, too. The techniques used to handle dominating participants in a workshop are the same as those described in leading group discussions.

Resolving disagreements

At times participants will have differing opinions about the categories in which some items should be placed. The first step in such disagreements is for a facilitator to always make sure that both perspectives are properly understood by all of the participants. Many times such disagreements are merely because of poor communication. The facilitator can also call for a third opinion from someone else in the group. If the disagreement still continues, the item can be set aside or "bracketed" until later. Additional information and subsequent discussions often help to clarify the relationship of the controversial items.

Group Consensus

The collective analysis of information moves toward a conclusion when participants name the various categories. The names emerge from the information that compose the categories, which is why it is important that names not be assigned until all information has been shared. By leaving the naming process until last, it is possible for fresh insights to be gleaned from all perspectives included in categories.

Participants can claim ownership of the resulting product of a workshop because they can trace their own unique contributions from the initial brainstorming session. They can see how their viewpoints are related to the overall analysis of the workshop topic. Reaching a consensus at this final stage is, however, a delicate process. Facilitators can benefit from a number of hints in the naming of categories.

Establish the broad arena of the category

The facilitator has the group quickly identify the general subject of the category. The name of the overarching theme is written in large letters and placed on the front wall for all to see.

The use of symbols is an effective way to mark similar ideas.

Determine the qualifying aspects of the category's name

Particular questions to discern the qualifying aspects of the title will depend upon the specific topic of the workshop. In a vision workshop, for example, a facilitator might ask a question like this to clarify anticipations about the category of water: "from all the information listed here, what is it that this community really hopes to accomplish in the next four or five years in regard to 'water'?" A good test for a proposed name is to check and see if every item in the category can comfortably remain under it. If not, then other names are tried.

Disagree to a proposed name by offering an alternative

Reaching a consensus on a name for a category is like buying a new suit of clothes. It's a matter of trial and error as the group "tries on" different names in order to see if they "fit." It is rarely the case that the first name proposed is the one that a group finally decides upon. When a name has been proposed, the facilitator never allows it to be rejected with a simple "no, that's not it." Disagreement is made by suggesting an alternative. It is through a series of possible alternative names that the group begins to clarify its own thinking.

Conclude the naming exercise with the "affirmative chorus"

Alternative suggestions for the name of the category continue to be offered until a consensus is reached. Most often this occurs through an "affirmative chorus" as many people say at once "yes, yes, that is it." When facilitators think that a consensus has been reached, they can ask a direct question to confirm if it has or not: "does this title communicate all that we intended with the information compiled in this category?"

Avoid voting

If the discussion about a name for a category bogs down in a disagreement between two different proposals, avoid the temptation to conduct a vote. **Voting always divides a group** and immediately creates winners on one side and losers on the other. Continue to seek other alternative names until a consensus has been reached.

Avoid naming categories until similar ideas have been put together.

Once names have been given to all of the categories, the workshop can be brought to a close by some concluding activity. In most participatory programmes, this is usually done (if time allows) by having the group reflect on the experience of doing the workshop. Following the techniques of leading a discussion, a series of brief objective, reflective, and interpretive questions are asked by the facilitator. If time is too short for such a discussion, then the facilitator can make a few concluding comments that honour the work of the participants and say something about the significance of the workshop product.

Presentation Techniques

Lecturing is generally considered to be a very poor approach to use in promoting participation. On occasions, however, it does become necessary to present information to groups of people. To avoid having **bored audiences**, it is important to find ways to keep presentations interesting and stimulating. Their preparation and delivery can be assisted through an assortment of creative techniques.

The preparation of a presentation can be done using the workshop method just described above. Begin by doing a "brainstorm" of all of the points that need to be included in the presentation. This is usually done by the one who will ultimately make the presentation, but ideas from others can also be solicited in the brainstorm.

Once the brainstorm has been completed, then organise the information into categories and name them. A helpful technique for organising a presentation is to decide upon the four basic points of the speech, and then determine the four sub-points under each one. A "4x4" will help create an underlying rationale for a presentation with sixteen key sub-points. The same can be done using a "3x3" format with nine sub-points, etc.

Presentations where someone merely stands up and talks about sixteen or nine points are rarely successful. People easily become bored when listening to someone drone on for a long time. Though there are many techniques to enhance public speaking, the following hints will assist in making presentations more lively and interesting.

Maintain a quick pace

Decide before making the presentation how long it should be. Then divide the time among the points. Some points will take more time and others less. Be strict with yourself in keeping to the schedule. Mark times on your notes so that you will be reminded about the pace you intend to keep.

Illustrate each point with a visual "image"

Simple diagrams, often including key words and other visual images drawn on a blackboard as you speak, will help your audience to both follow your presentation and to remember it afterwards. It is a good discipline to create a visual image for each of the sixteen (or nine) sub-points. Visuals should be clear and straightforward and not overly mysterious and in need of a lot of explanation. Test them out by showing them to a friend or colleague without explaining them and ask what they seem to convey. After receiving their comments, discuss what you had hoped to communicate. This should assist you in adjusting the images for more effective use in your presentation.

Voting always divides a group into winners and losers.

Tell a "life experience" as an example for each key point

Story-telling is always an important part of making interesting presentations. Without examples from real life experiences, the points in a presentation tend to remain abstract and theoretical. Most people would readily agree in principle if a speaker said "rural women are practical thinkers and should be more involved in decision-making," but an example illustrating the point would be more effective:

> The women of Mupizwa were pleased when the village council decided to build a new school. Many young children had been kept at home because it was too far for them to walk to the neighbouring village to attend the ward school. But they were upset when they learned that the leaders, all who were men, had decided to devote an entire week, Monday through Friday, to building the new school. How could crops be attended and other ongoing work completed? After discussing among themselves, the women suggested that every Friday for an entire month should be set aside for a village-wide work-day. Once this idea was put forward to the leaders, it was quickly adopted.

Have the audience contribute through questions and answers

The more interaction between the presenter and the audience, the better. This can be accomplished through the use of short questions and answers at strategic moments in your presentation. The point above might be amplified in a presentation by asking "can someone else give another example of why it is important to involve women in village decisions?" Once an example has been given, continue with the next point.

Conclusion

Group discussions, workshops, and visual presentations will help facilitators as they promote participatory activities. The practical techniques described in this chapter can assist development programmes of all types realise their ambitions to involve rural people in the planning of development projects. These techniques are further examined in light of different steps of the project cycle in Chapter 14. But now we turn to considering the indirect details that are so important in establishing a conducive environment for participatory planning.

Chapter 13

FACTORS FOR CREATING A PARTICIPATORY ENVIRONMENT

The general atmosphere in which planning events take place is as crucial to effective participation as are sound techniques for leading discussions and facilitating workshops. "STEPS" points to five important programme dimensions which can create a good environment: space, time, eventfulness, product, and style.

Space

Participation seminars have occurred in almost every conceivable space. They have been held in classrooms, meeting halls, storerooms, churches, and under trees. But the successful use of these depends upon proper preparation and careful arrangements. Before a seminar actually takes place, facilitators visit the proposed venue during the set-up meeting and review a checklist of the following points.

Can the space comfortably accommodate all participants?

The venue needs to be large enough to comfortably seat all of the participants. If the space is too small, participants will feel cramped and unwelcome. Similarly, if the venue is too large, groups can spread out into an indefinite sprawl. A way must be found to divide off an area from the larger space in order to consolidate discussions.

How will the participants sit?

Are tables and chairs available in sufficient numbers? If school desks are to be used, are they large enough to seat adults? If meeting outdoors, are benches or logs available? Is the area adequately grassy so that people can comfortably sit on the ground? The host community will likely have established meeting places where these problems have already been solved, but facilitators visit the venues and consider these questions.

Can written results from teams be easily displayed during plenaries?

Summary statements from team discussions need to be displayed during reports to plenaries. Does the venue easily allow for this to happen? If tape is to be used with papers and cards, does it stick firmly to the walls or does it easily fall to the floor? Can chalk be easily seen on the blackboards? Is a large easel required? An easel is usually a necessity if the meeting occurs in the outdoors. Are any other special arrangements needed to allow for an easy display of reports?

Is there adequate space for both small teams and group plenaries?

Space is needed for small teams to work separately. These spaces need to be nearby the meeting area for the large group so that time is not wasted moving about, but far enough away that discussions can occur in quiet surroundings.

Plan the seating arrangement according to the venue

The best seating arrangement for large groups is a modification of the UN style. Tables and chairs are arranged to face in three directions with the front of the room reserved for the display of reports and the front table for the facilitator. The traditional classroom arrangement where students sit in rows and face the teacher is avoided at all costs. The same is true for traditional seating arrangements in churches. The seating arrangements for small teams can be in circles.

Time

Facilitators make good use of time. The effective management of time is one of the essential elements that make for successful participation programmes. Below are some particular considerations that demand attention in regard to time.

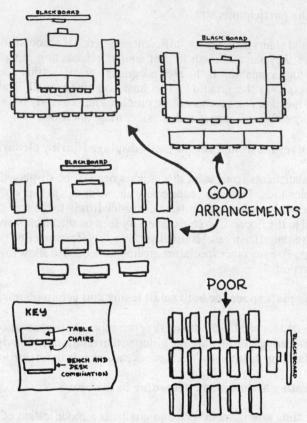

Illustrate key points in a presentation with a visual image.

Scheduling in awareness of the agricultural season

Peak times for planting, cultivating, and harvesting crops are poor times to schedule popular participation events in the rural countryside. These are particularly difficult times for women to attend meetings. Facilitators make careful work-plans by identifying busy agricultural seasons and avoid scheduling planning events during those times.

Punctual arrival of facilitators

Facilitators can enthusiastically declare that villagers are important and have valuable contributions to make in formal seminars, but if they arrive late and make villagers wait, then a much different message is communicated. The late arrival of facilitators reinforces an old image that says village people are of low importance. Good facilitators strive to communicate a genuine esteem for villagers in all that they do and remember wisdom from the ages: actions speak louder than words.

Pacing of the sessions

All steps in the planning process do not require an equal division of time. The four levels of questions used in group discussions, for example, are seldom given equal time. Objective questions and reflective questions can usually be answered much faster than interpretive or decisional questions. Facilitating a workshop is like running a long-distance race: the trick is in knowing when to slow down and when to speed up. Time estimates are carefully made when the workshop is prepared and provide a facilitator with a guideline for pacing time on each question and topic. Distractions that cause a session to drag, like long repetitive "speeches" from some of the vocal participants, are carefully watched and dealt with when they occur.

Eventfulness

Boredom, when it occurs, undermines participatory planning. Facilitators work to keep sessions exciting and interesting. The content of discussions, of course, must ultimately keep participants actively engaged, but a good workshop builds in additional means to nurture the active interest of participants.

Maintain a balance between various group activities

Variety is the spice of life. This is just as true in facilitating workshops as it is in other dimensions of everyday living. Good planning sessions balance the emphasis between discussions, workshops, and presentations. Participants need to work alone as individuals, work together in small teams, and participate in large plenary discussions. Variance of space is also important. Moving from one room to another is an excellent way to occasion a transition in the planning process.

Techniques for keeping participants engaged

Small teams are asked to make reports to the plenary gatherings on many occasions. It is a good idea to have these reports made by as many different people as possible rather than allowing one person to emerge as the team's spokesperson. Similarly, when questions are asked from the group, a

Sitting arrangements should allow participants to see each other.

facilitator can call on different participants in the team to answer. A facilitator can also ask teams to sit together and have mini-discussions during plenary sessions: "which proposal from your teamwork is the most bold and challenging? discuss among yourselves to select one from your list." This keeps everyone involved even though all may not speak publicly to the whole group.

The use of humour

Discussions become more interesting when people enjoy themselves through common laughter. Humour can be used very effectively in facilitating planning sessions. Though prepared jokes can sometimes work, spontaneous humour emerging from comments in the discussions is usually more effective. The chief caution is to be sure that the humour never belittles a participant. Humour is usually used in the early parts of a session. As discussions become more intense, which makes them interesting for other reasons, humour is out of place. A light humorous comment while participants are wrestling with a deep and painful problem in their community is obviously inappropriate.

Celebrating a group's output

When teams present their proposals, other participants often want to demonstrate their approval. These are at times for the specific content of suggestions and ideas while they are at other times for the team's effort. Affirmations by applause, ululation, or other means are common in rural Africa and often occur quite spontaneously. Facilitators can also call for these at strategic intervals to enliven the sessions. Songs are also often appropriate.

Product

Specific products resulting from participation planning seminars heighten a group's sense of accomplishment. Far too often, participants leave interesting discussions only to have conclusions and decisions fade into vague memories because no tangible products were ever produced.

Explain the anticipated product during introductions to workshops

Participants can more confidently enter into discussions when the destination of the session has been clearly stated. People want to know the objective of their talk. Explaining the end-product of the session also helps to keep discussions on track. Products of workshops can be decisions and plans that are then recorded in some practical form like written reports.

Visual displays

The final product of most planning exercises are printed reports. Many people in the rural countryside, however, are illiterate. Products may also be produced in the visual form of pictures, charts, or diagrams. Visual renderings of plans and decisions are very practical ways to enable everyone to participate in receiving the final product.

Summary charts in the written reports

The drawing of summary charts of workshops is a helpful way of presenting workshop results. Charts can summarise all of the information from a workshop on a single piece of paper. They also can illustrate complex relationships of information at a glance. Organising the results of an obstacles workshop in chart form by adapting a simple bar graph–places different categories in a perspective with one another. A written report, important as it is for elaborating upon explanatory details, requires many pages (and much time to read) in order to communicate the same relationships.

Quick distribution of the workshop product

The final product of a participatory workshop—be it a chart, decision statement, or a long written report—embodies the contributions and commitments of participants. The sooner results are distributed after a workshop the better they can mark a sense of significant accomplishment for the time expended in the planning sessions. In almost all circumstances it is possible to produce some form of a product before participants leave a planning seminar. Many programmes present a large wall chart with visual pictures of projects to local leaders in an impromptu "closing ceremony" for the seminar. Others that have access to mimeograph machines even produce summary charts of all the sessions and then distribute copies to every participant before they go home.

A wall-chart can even be presented at the end of the seminar.

If written reports are produced by facilitators later when they return to the office, every attempt should be made to ensure that they are quickly distributed after the completion of the seminar.

Style

The personal style of a facilitator probably does as much as anything to establish a comfortable working environment conducive for participatory programmes. Some people, of course, seem to be born with charm and grace while others have to work at it. Below are some ways of developing helpful stylistic qualities of a facilitator.

Honouring individual contributions

Facilitators are affirmative of participants' work. They receive all answers and assume that wisdom lies behind every contribution. This is true for items that may even appear to be superficial or shallow on first reading. It is the responsibility of the facilitators to ask sensitive questions that enable deeper thinking. These questions are asked with respect and communicate a sincere desire to discover basic insights. The work of individual participants is thus honoured by a facilitator's serious questions.

Honouring the group

Facilitators honour the group by attending to everything that villagers have to say. Quite simply, facilitators pay attention. This is as true when they are sitting at the side of the room as it is when they are leading discussions up front. Inattention communicates a disinterest in participants' ideas. Casually reading a newspaper while villagers struggle to build a plan for their future degrades the significance of the participants' work. It says a facilitator really isn't interested and "couldn't care less" about their plans.

Demonstrating the power of teamwork

Facilitators operate as a team and are a demonstration of the power of effective teamwork to villagers. Even when not actually leading discussions, a facilitator is always ready to assist in any appropriate way. They are taking notes and asking appropriate questions from the side of the room if discussions bog down. Facilitators also develop their skills from watching one another and receiving the constructive criticism of others. Staff self-evaluations are a part of the job. This, of course, is not possible if facilitators are not attentively following discussions and taking notes.

Intervening in confrontations or domination

Facilitators play a mediating role when discussions slide into a confrontation between personalities. They do this by objectifying differing perspectives and acknowledging the insights of each. Dominating participants can also slow down progress in discussions. Facilitators maintain a style that politely calls this into question for the sake of the entire group.

Facilitators avoid the trappings of a "visiting VIP"

The aim of facilitators is to empower ordinary villagers and encourage them to become self-confident and self-reliant. Care is taken by facilitators to demonstrate an identification with villagers. Though they dress with clean clothes and are never sloppy in appearance, they avoid overdressing. Female facilitators avoid wearing fancy hair-dos that often offend rural sensibilities.

Special treatment is neither expected nor sought. Even the small and subtle symbols of a visiting VIP are shunned: they refrain from keeping participants waiting as they make a "grand entrance"; they mix freely with participants and engage in friendly conversation during the breaks from the formal sessions; facilitators avoid taking the important-looking chairs that sit above participants.

Conclusion

Creating a participatory environment for conducting a programme is extremely important. The biggest messages are often communicated in the smallest details. Facilitators take care in managing space, time, eventfulness, product, and style.

Chapter 14

ENSURING QUALITY IN THE
PLANNING PROCESS

As was seen in Chapter 10, MAP utilises a number of techniques to enable broad participation in the planning and implementation of rural development projects. This chapter examines ways to ensure a high degree of quality in the different steps of the "project cycle" when using MAP methods. Exciting discussions and enthusiastic workshops are utterly useless if the results end in poor-quality plans.

Many aspects of the project cycle take place during short-term MAP "seminars" when participants are engaged in workshops concerning vision, obstacles, proposals, project selection, and implementation plans. This is usually preceded by the collection of "base-line data" during a set-up meeting with village leaders. Once plans have been made in MAP seminars, facilitators continue to "monitor" progress on local projects through a series of visits and follow-up meetings. "Evaluation" is an important part of any project work. With MAP, participatory evaluations often re-initiate the entire process all over again.

A specific section of the present chapter is devoted to each step of the project cycle. Problems and difficulties of applying MAP techniques to each step are discussed and various suggestions are made for ways that facilitators might overcome them. Several examples are also provided as models of good-quality results.

Before turning to these sections on the project cycle, a reminder about the importance of reporting to officials. The focus of MAP work is with ordinary rural people, but permission for it to take place often comes from officials sitting far away in city centres. Many a good programme has been derailed because it was misunderstood by senior government officials. It is crucial, therefore, that facilitators keep officials informed about the progress of their activities.

Contact with appropriate authorities begins in the set-up phase. Presentation meetings are arranged to discuss plans and review anticipated work schedules. Contact continues through submission of reports from village workshops. Remember, it is far better to err by keeping officials "over informed" than risk the wrath of an official who feels "under informed."

Once contact has been made with all necessary officials, facilitators are then ready to begin their actual work in the rural areas.

The Current Situation

The starting-point for any serious planning is a review of the current situation. This is important for several reasons. First, it is educational for the facilitators. When facilitators go to conduct planning seminars, they need to be familiar with the history and concerns of a community so they can be conversant with participants and anticipate possible problem areas when discussing project feasibility.

Second, a review of the current situation is also educational for participants. It is a mistake to assume that local residents are readily familiar with current development activities in the community. Though a few people may have such information, it may not be widely known. A review of the current situation will help to establish a common starting-point for the planning exercise.

Third, participation programmes are often accountable to donors who expect regular progress reports. Government officials also need to know about programme results. A serious analysis of impact without base-line data from the start of a programme is impossible. The use of standardized questionnaires is a good way to collect base-line data. They objectify the situation within a community and provide a basis for marking progress and change.

Questionnaires for the collection of base-line information can be of varying degrees of complexity. A good guideline for facilitators is this: use a simple questionnaire that obtains important information and then be scrupulously disciplined in faithfully collecting correct data from every community where the programme is conducted. It is easy to design a questionnaire that seeks too much information. Good reliable information on a few points is much better than sloppy information on many points.

Careful attention needs to be given to designing the base-line questionnaire when a participation programme begins. Facilitators and donors need to discuss important information and agree upon a common format. Below are some of the possible items that a questionnaire might include.

Population

In addition to total number of males and females, sub-categories can also be asked: number of children, boys and girls, as defined by a particular age; elderly men and women, again defined by a specific age; numbers of able bodied and disabled. If possible, record the date that information of the population was collected.

Publicly owned facilities by the local community

A questionnaire can include a list of typical facilities (schools, health clinic, shop, tractor, access roads, milling machine, storage building) where the number of each is recorded. The condition of these facilities can also be noted (1 = in good working order, 2 = fair condition, 3 = not working). The questionnaire can leave blank space to add other facilities not included on the list.

Privately owned facilities within the community

This category might use the same questions as above but focuses on those facilities that are privately owned.

Sources of personal income and livelihood

In agricultural areas, this is largely a matter of listing food crops, cash crops, livestock, handicrafts, and other sources of income. Since most questionnaires seek information from the community as a whole, these are general estimates rather than specific data from particular households.

Availability of extension services

Information regarding extension work helps provide a picture of government support to an area. The questionnaire might include a list of possible extension services (agriculture, health, community development, cooperatives, other) so that information can be collected on their availability. Opinions can also be obtained about their quality (good, fair, inadequate).

Completed development projects in the past

Since many participation programmes seek to encourage a renewal of self-help activities, it is very important to obtain information on past development projects within the community. Past projects are listed and the following information collected for each: date the project began, date completed, institution(s) which provided any assistance, the specific nature of assistance (amount of money, etc), results, and implementation problems encountered while doing the project.

Status of current development projects

Questions concerning current projects within the community are the same with space for recording an anticipated date of completion. This information, along with that from past projects, provides a context for understanding any future project activities that might be undertaken as a result of planning from the seminar. It also informs facilitators about the feasibility of any proposals for future projects.

Additional items are added or substituted depending upon the particular focus of the participation programme. For example, programmes working with cooperatives might collect information to provide a profile about the services of the local co-op society. Questions might be asked about crop purchases, amount of the annual financial turnover, quantities of fertilizers and pesticides provided to members, etc.

Once the questionnaire has been completed, it becomes the first major piece of information that facilitators place into a newly opened file for the community. This file is subsequently kept up-to-date by adding information after every contact with the community.

Practical Vision

Declaring a "vision" for where a community or organisation intends to go in the future is an important step in any planning process. As the old proverb says, "where there is no vision, the people perish."

Vision statements are most exciting when they articulate people's true aspirations, are concrete and specific, and (while attainable) are beyond immediate reach. Bold vision challenges people to stretch themselves to transform their dreams into reality; it inspires and motivates. Unity comes from a shared commitment to such a common vision.

Vision workshops in MAP begin by asking participants to imagine themselves standing five years in the future and describe what they see. "What are the realistic hopes and dreams you have for this community?" This is the brainstorm question. Participants are reminded that their answers need to be practical and realistic and as specific as possible. When the information from the brainstorms is organised, the criterion for putting items together is a "similar accomplishment."

The initial vision brainstorm from workshop participants often varies in quality. Though most vision items usually reflect genuine aspirations, the statements are sometimes general and abstract. It is the responsibility of the facilitator to push for deeper thinking, especially when vision categories are named from the brainstorm data. Below are some typical problems that often arise while conducting a vision workshop and possible ways that a facilitator can respond.

Unrealistic "dreaming"

Some participants tend to treat the vision brainstorm as a game and suggest ideas that are completely unrealistic. A vision to "build a big hospital" in a village is probably not offered as a serious suggestion. Some participants like to joke by being "grandiose." Facilitators can treat such responses in the spirit they were given, humorously, and put them to the side. But if suggested in all seriousness, the facilitator affirms the contribution while asking about its feasibility. As with many problems, it is best to anticipate possible confusion and handle it before people do their personal brainstorming. A clear reminder in the introduction that all items should be realistic will be helpful.

Special care needs to be given to the use of local language. For a long time, theKiswahili word **ndoto** was used to ask the vision question in rural Tanzania. Only later was it learned that **ndoto** communicated a sense of a "fantastic dream." It is not surprising, therefore, that brainstorm items tended to be frivolous and unrealistic. The situation was eventually corrected by the use of a more appropriate Kiswahili word, **mpango**, meaning "future development projects."

Short-term thinking

In the opposite direction, vision items can also be too specific and immediate. It is hard to believe that "two acres of pigeon peas" really conveys the full depth of a youth's aspiration for the future of the village. Again, anticipating this problem and clarifying the purpose of the brainstorm before people do their individual thinking is the best way to deal with it. If such items come up when organising information during the workshop, they are never rejected: all are a clue to the true vision of the community. The facilitator can ask, "why are two acres of pigeon peas important? what would they help to accomplish in the long-term future of the community?"

Such short-term, immediate items from brainstorm lists is not a big problem because they can always be combined with other items that point toward the long-term future. But it is important that the final names decided upon as titles for different categories of the vision avoid being too immediate and specific. Vision names need to declare the bold challenges that the community wishes to set for itself: "school buildings within walking distance for every child."

Abstract statements

The most typical problem encountered in vision workshops is one of abstraction. Hopes and dreams are stated so vaguely that they become mere indicators of a broad, general direction thereby losing the compelling power of a bold, concrete vision. Initial brainstorm items can be somewhat abstract without causing too much of a problem, but it is important that facilitators enable the final names for vision categories to be more concrete.

Abstract statements can be transformed into specific vision titles by asking "what would we see if this was to happen?" Take, for example, a statement about "improved health." A facilitator might ask "if we were to return in five years and take a picture of new developments in health care, **what would we see in the photographs**?" Caution would have to be maintained to keep the responses realistic; it is doubtful if most rural villages can establish their own dispensary and clinic with a doctor. Realistic answers might include "pit latrines in every home" and "education classes in sanitation and hygiene," etc.

Below are some typical abstract vision statements followed by some statements that are more concrete and substantial. These are merely examples and are not intended to be "right answers." Every group will have its own unique perspective on its vision. The examples do, however, enable a new facilitator to become familiar with the difference between statements that are abstract and those that have substance. Remember, a good vision statement clearly describes a reality that can be seen.

Vision "Abstractions"	Vision of "Substance"
• improved transportation	• new trailer for tractor
• more cooperation	• village-wide work-days
• modern farming techniques	• terraces on hillsides
• good health	• pit latrines in every home
• increased production	• introduction of grade cattle
• new sources of income	• opening of a new tea-shop
• better education	• new teacher in science class

Obstacles

Obstacle statements describe the underlying causes that are preventing the vision from being realised. Just as weeds in the fields must be pulled by their roots, obstacles, too, have root causes which must be addressed if they are to be overcome. Though obstacles are often referred to as "problems," they are really windows to the future showing a group where they need to move.

The obstacle workshop begins by clarifying the question for the brainstorm: "what is blocking this community from realising its vision?" Though a facilitator tries to have participants look deeply at the issues, much of the information generated in the brainstorm will be irritations and immediate problems. Doctors use symptoms of an illness to diagnose a disease. Similarly, facilitators use these surface perceptions to guide participants in a search for root causes. A "root cause" is the criteria for putting together problems from the brainstorm. The final names given to obstacle categories reflect the insights from this search beneath the surface.

Below are some typical problems that a facilitator might encounter while conducting an obstacle workshop and possible ways to resolve them.

The given situation

Often participants say "drought" or "famine" or the "failure of the rains" are their problem. These general statements imply problems over which participants have no control. Obstacles, however, reveal particular practices and life patterns over which participants can exercise a degree of control. When general-situation statements are offered as obstacles, facilitators can ask questions to reveal the human causes that may lie beneath these problems: "overgrazing by livestock, poor cultivation practices, inadequate storage of crops from the previous harvest," etc.

Insufficient money

"Lack of money" is one of the most frequent items to appear in brainstorming sessions on obstacles. But insufficient funds is a surface reading of the problem. After all, most communities will never reach a point when people will be satisfied with available funds. The challenge of the facilitator is to ask questions that enable participants to look beyond the surface toward the contributing causes for a shortage of funds over which they have some control: "poor financial planning, unprioritized expenditures, unaccountable use of funds, untapped opportunities for income generation," etc.

"Lack of ..." statements

Obstacles are real problems that are blocking progress toward the vision like a fallen tree in the road. They are not empty phantoms as "lack of" statements seem to imply. When boarding a rural commuter bus in the rain, a passenger sees very concrete problems: bald tyres, broken windshield wipers, and unmarked roads rather than a "lack of safety." If participants say "lack of" something is a problem, facilitators can enable concrete statements to emerge by asking about the underlying causes.

Superficial problems

A good technique to enable a group to think deeper about obstacles is to repeatedly ask the question "what is stopping you from realising your vision?" The question can be asked over and over again until the group answers "nothing, we just have to decide." The following is an example of questions from a facilitator and responses from participants:

Q: You said "increased productivity" on your farms is a part of your vision. What is stopping you from having increased productivity on your farms?
A: Lack of education.
Q: What kind of education do you need?
A: Training in modern techniques of agriculture.
Q: What is stopping you from having agricultural training?
A: No training days are ever scheduled in this village.
Q: What is stopping you from scheduling training days?
A: The agricultural extension officer never visits this village.
Q: What is stopping the extension officer from making visits?
A: She is afraid she will be robbed or attacked by animals when walking alone on the road through the forest.
Q: What is stopping you from accompanying her through the forest on her way to your village?
A: Nothing, we just have to decide.

When participants arrive at saying "nothing is stopping us, we just have to decide," a tangible root problem is usually revealed. Participants can then take practical steps to solve it. Knowing that the extension officer does not visit the village for fear of being robbed or attacked by wild animals is more revealing than "lack of education."

Below are some examples of shallow obstacle statements and some more revealing counterparts. As before, these provide facilitators with some illustrations of good obstacle statements and are not meant to be definitive of every group's experience.

"Superficial"	"Underlying" Obstacles
• lack of education	• poor publicity of literacy class
• not enough money	• unaccountable use of funds
• selfishness	• few benefits of co-op membership
• floods	• deforestation & overgrazing
• poor management	• late ordering of fertilizers
• lack of cooperation	• irregularly called meetings

Proposals

The proposals workshop has participants consider the question "how can these obstacle be overcome, by-passed, or eliminated?" Answers from the brainstorm explore different ways that the big underlying problems can be solved. This is the first step toward making plans for future action.

Proposals differ from the "vision" in a number of ways. Vision focuses on long-term aspirations while proposals focus on resolving problems. Five years is a usual time-frame for vision while proposals are more immediate and made for only one or two years. Information from the vision brainstorm is organised by "similar accomplishments" while the criteria for combining proposal items is the sharing of a "common intent." When proposal categories are named, they point out the strategic directions in which the community needs to move.

The most typical problem encountered in facilitating a proposals workshop is the tendency of participants to make recommendations for other groups and agencies. With the proposals, participants are creating a plan for themselves; it is not a planning workshop for what someone else should do! It is important for facilitators to remind participants of this fact before they do their brainstorm. The question they consider is "what can WE do to overcome the obstacles that are preventing US from realising OUR vision?"

Project Selection

Vision, obstacles, and proposals are steps where participants consider the "big picture" about development activities in their community. They are important to the planning process for two reasons: 1) they create a common picture about the community and where it needs to go and 2) they build a sense of confidence among participants that the planning process is on the right track. Yet they only set the stage for the planning of more specific activities. After all, people cannot usually go out and directly do a "vision."

Identifying self-help projects for short-term implementation is, therefore, an important turning-point in MAP seminars. For it is in this workshop that practical activities are planned. The question participants are asked to consider is "what small projects can we do with the use of local resources that would start us on our journey towards realising our long-term vision?" This question is usually discussed in small teams where projects are suggested and closely examined. Rather than organising these suggestions into broad categories, the recommended projects are carefully reviewed and then selected in the following plenary session.

Below are some helpful guidelines that will assist a facilitator when conducting a workshop for identifying self-help projects.

Consider many possibilities

A brainstorm is important for generating a lot of ideas about possible projects. There is a temptation in many groups to quickly agree upon the very first projects that are proposed. Before discussing which projects to choose, a facilitator completes the brainstorm by having every participant contribute an idea. Once many ideas have been suggested, then the group can begin to consider the strengths and weaknesses of each proposed project and make a selection based on their responses.

Consider the "feasibility" of the projects

Before deciding to do a project, participants need to carefully consider its feasibility. Is the project really likely to succeed? A facilitator can lead a brief conversation that quickly examines questions like these:

> what resources will be required to do this project?
> how might these resources be obtained?
> what past experience do you have with this type of project?
> what is the likelihood of overcoming past problems?
> what are the prospects for finding a market?
> is there real cause to think you can make sales?
> what conditions are required for the project to succeed?
> why is it realistic to think that this project can succeed?
> would it be better to leave this project for a later time?

Name an "anticipated accomplishment"

Once a project has been broadly determined, specific objectives of the project need to be stated in an "anticipated accomplishment." A good guideline is to always have participants assign a number to the project, thereby establishing an "anticipated accomplishment." By quantifying the project, participants begin to consider practical tasks involved in working on the project and provide themselves with an easy way to measure progress and results. For example, "poultry production" is a general title for a project but "establish and maintain 100 layers" makes it much more specific.

Discuss the "ownership" of the project

When planning community development projects, it is important to establish the ownership of the project. Ownership has to do with project control either in regard to future decisions or distribution of benefits. If not specifically asked, participants may simply assume that the ownership of the project is commonly understood only to learn later, when benefits are to be distributed, that many different perspectives were held on the subject. Deciding upon ownership during the planning phase will help avoid disagreements later on.

Some communities decide that the ownership of the project should be by a special group or "club" rather than the general community as an unspecified whole. When ownership of the project is to be by the formation of a special "club," some good questions for a facilitator to ask are:

> how will membership to this club be determined?
> how will this club make decisions?
> how is money to be handled and accounted for?
> how will any surpluses be distributed?
> how often will the club membership meet?

Implementation Plans

Implementation planning is deciding the "who, where, when, and how" of actually working on a project. Participants usually attend small team discussions to plan these steps according to personal interest. The results of these implementation plans are then shared in the plenary session. Below are some practical guidelines which will assist a facilitator in leading discussions on implementation planning.

Implementation steps of "substance"

Community groups often tend to plan vague empty procedural steps when planning implementation activities: 1) form a works committee, 2) the committee meets and plans, 3) the committee reports to officials, 4) work on the project is then organised and carried out. Such steps do not constitute a plan. They merely describe a contentless process.

location:
  date:

IMPLEMENTATION PLANNING WORK SHEET

name of the self-help project:

what materials
are needed?

what tools are
required?

how will these
be gathered?

how much money
will be needed?

how will this
money be raised?

what skilled
labour is
required?

what general
labour is
needed?

how will
this labour
be organised?

when will the
work take place?

who will be the   men   women
coordinators? 1-   1-
                         2-   2-

Implementation plans identify all of the practical tasks which must be accomplished if a project is to be successfully completed. Materials must be arranged, tools gathered, and work-days organised. Sometimes money needs to be collected. Coordinators need to be designated. An example of a work-sheet is shown for planning implementation steps. If participants do not have access to such work-sheets, then facilitators can guide the discussions by asking the same questions.

Seasonal considerations for scheduling

The scheduling of implementation steps needs to be carefully considered in light of other demands on people's time. In the rural areas, this is connected to the seasons for crop planting, cultivation, and harvesting. Before scheduling work on the projects, a facilitator has participants review the agricultural seasons of the area. Once peak times have been identified and marked on a calendar, then implementation activities are scheduled by the participants at times that avoid the busy rush of the agricultural work.

Selection of project coordinators

Coordinators are not responsible for doing all of the work themselves; it is their job to organise the work and ensure that people are involved and preparations are made. Coordinators need to work as a team thereby providing each other with mutual support and accountability. In planning large projects involving both men and women, it is a good idea to name both male and female coordinators. In such circumstances, it is best to have men and women named in pairs: one woman assigned alone sometimes has difficulties working as a coordinator with a man because the man will often take a strong lead.

Monitoring and Evaluation

The planning of projects is one thing; actually bringing self-help projects to successful fruition is something altogether different. The wise facilitator never underestimates the need for continued monitoring of projects or self-evaluation with participants. Most of the participation programmes using MAP follow a specific routine of regular monitoring visits and follow-up meetings after completing a planning seminar. Below are some ideas that will assist facilitators in their monitoring and evaluation work.

Written reports and record keeping

Good monitoring depends to a large extent on good record-keeping. This is true for both the facilitators who are promoting participation and the villagers who are implementing their own projects.

Most MAP seminars end with the presentation of a large wall-chart depicting the community's plan to be posted in a prominent location. The chart includes all essential information: names of designated projects, implementation schedules, and the names of project coordinators. An image of each project is also drawn on the chart so that illiterate members of the community can also know about the projects planned during the seminar.

A wall-chart is an immediate way to record plans from the seminar. A more thorough report on the community plan is prepared by the facilitators once they return to their office. These reports are then distributed to the seminar participants and to all authorities who are overseeing the programme. These reports are a summary of seminar discussions on vision, obstacles, proposals, self-help projects, and implementation plans.

Facilitators keep an open file on each community where they work. The written report on the community plans joins the base-line data which was collected prior to the holding of the seminar. As follow-up meetings and monitoring visits occur, all information concerning progress on the projects and discussions about overcoming any implementation problems are also added to the files.

Record-keeping by village participants

Locally kept records are very important if a group is to monitor its own progress. Such records can be maintained in a number of different ways. For example, if eggs have begun to be produced and marketed as a part of a poultry project, then sales information can be drawn in chart form and posted for everyone's review. Then every month it can be updated to indicate the condition of the project. Facilitators assist in creating these kinds of simple materials so that local participants can observe and evaluate their own progress.

Monitoring visits by facilitators

Facilitators often make informal "monitoring visits" to the groups following the conclusion of planning seminars. On these occasions project progress is discussed with leaders and other participants in a spontaneous setting. The purpose of monitoring visits is the same as with more formal follow-up meetings: encouraging participants in their project work and discussing ways to overcome any potential problems that might be causing projects to stall. Once back to the office, this information enables the facilitators to up-date their own records.

Formal follow-up meetings

Typically, a three or four hour "follow-up" meeting takes place on three-month intervals where all of the participants from the seminar return to discuss progress on their projects. These meetings are "participatory evaluations" where information on each project is shared. Participants review project problems and discuss ways that they might be overcome. The next stage of project implementation is then planned by arranging work-days, materials, tools, organisation, and coordination, etc, in a similar fashion to implementation planning of the original seminar. Depending upon the nature of the group and its projects, other topics, e.g. finance reports, creation of group by-laws, etc, are also discussed during follow-up meetings.

By-laws for newly formed groups

When special "clubs" have been formed to implement a community project, it is good to include time in a follow-up meeting to review the group's operating rules, or "by-laws." These can include the same questions about club membership, decision-making, and distribution of benefits that were raised during the planning of the project in the original seminar. Time can also be given to write up these operating guidelines if they have not been published.

Finance reports

Financial reporting is often a weak point in small-scale rural projects. By calling for a finance report in a follow-up meeting, the facilitators reaffirm the need to keep everyone in the community up-to-date on financial matters. This report can be very basic: how much money has been collected in regard to the project, what expenses have occurred, and what is the current balance? Additional questions from the participants in response to these points will further clarify the situation.

Physical inspection of the projects

During both formal follow-up meetings and more informal monitoring visits, it is a good idea for facilitators to make a physical inspection of the projects. Physical inspections also enable the facilitators to make their own judgements about the real progress of the project. For whatever reason, participants often tend to exaggerate their accomplishments. Viewing a project can enable facilitators to ask participants more specific questions pertaining to the implementation work.

Monitoring and follow-up meetings need to include time for financial reports.

Maintaining a "tracking chart"

The more communities with whom a facilitation team is working, the more difficult it is to keep track of all the various activities that need to take place with each community. Once the intended routine of monitoring visits and follow-up meetings has been determined, they can be displayed on a large "tracking chart" placed on the office wall. This chart is a valuable tool for creating the facilitators' work schedule and for ensuring that all follow-up activities occur at the appropriate time.

Planning new projects

Most self-help projects in rural areas can be successfully launched, if not actually completed, within a year. The planning cycle is brought to full circle as the completed projects help establish a new situation from which future plans are made. Rather than starting again from scratch, "participatory evaluation" events that occur a year after an original seminar can quickly review the contents of previous discussions. These will reveal where adjustments in vision, obstacles, and proposals need to be made according to progress made and any new views from the participants.

It is only at the point of selecting new projects that significant new plans will most likely need to be formulated. This can be accomplished by repeating the same seminar workshops to choose projects and plan implementation steps.

Conclusion

This chapter has focused on techniques for ensuring quality thinking among participants in planning seminars. It has reviewed problems and provided examples for every step of the planning process. If facilitators are to succeed in enabling participants to think deeply, then they themselves need to have a very good understanding of the essential elements of quality plans. This is the first requirement of a good facilitator.

Good facilitation, however, also requires the ability to guide a group through a **journey of discovery**. Practically speaking, this means that facilitators need to place different emphasis on different points during the course of a seminar. Though facilitators need to be able to recognise good, solid vision statements, the vision workshop is probably not the best place to push hard for good-quality statements when most participants are still timid and unaccustomed to the participatory process. They most likely need to have their contributions affirmed rather than challenged. Later, once they have become familiar with the process, they can be pushed to deeper thinking as they plan particular projects.

This chapter has presented a number of suggestions describing how a facilitator might ensure deep thinking on the part of participants. The sensitivity for knowing **when** to push for deeper thinking is, however, just as important as knowing **how**. That sensitivity largely develops through experience and careful reflection and self-evaluation.

When using MAP methods to design new participation programmes, it is important to prepare specific procedures for workshops and seminars. These procedures are detailed "scripts" that inform facilitators about the intended flow of the sessions. The descriptions about the CMPP, IRDP, and LAMP seminars above are not scripted procedures. They are far too general. In procedural scripts time allotments are assigned to each step; every point of every workshop is spelled out; specific questions are prepared for every discussion; notes are made on the use of materials. Every detail is given attention. Such written procedures then become the facilitators' "bible" as they go out to conduct the participation seminars.

Printed procedures, even when in the greatest of detail, are no substitute for a facilitator's own personal handwritten notes. Good facilitators prepare for each workshop by writing up their own procedures and phrasing questions and comments according to their own style. This personal preparation helps to acquaint facilitators with the procedures of the workshop and thereby develop a sense of self-confidence about their performance before groups.

The best of procedures, however, only serve as guidelines for conducting seminars. Stale questions parroted mindlessly from the "blueprint" of printed procedures will not realise the aims of MAP. Good facilitators clearly understand WHY they are asking the questions they do and LISTEN to the answers they receive as they respond accordingly.

Creative, flexible interaction with participants emerges from a comfortable familiarity with the procedures. Disciplined adherence to the procedures followed by careful reflection and regular evaluation with other facilitators will eventually bear fruit as facilitators develop a sense of self-confidence about their work.

The key to developing good facilitation skills and a sensitivity to participants is thus through old-fashioned hard work. Such is the journey of facilitators as they move toward fulfilling their calling: to enable rural people to become agents of their own development.

MAP AND CMPP DOCUMENTATION

Terry Bergdall:

"Training Facilitators in Participation Promotion Programmes," a paper presented at the 'Regional Conference on the Promotion of Popular Participation in Rural Development Projects,' in Siavonga, Institute for African Studies, University of Zambia, October 1991.

"Draft Procedures for 'Inventory and Maintenance Committee Planning Workshop,'" presented to the IRDP/EP, September 1991.

"Project Design for 'Village Environmental Planning Seminars,'" presented to the Babati LAMP, April 1991.

"Report on the Constituency Participation Seminars in the Babati Land Management Programme," April 1991.

"The Branch Maintenance Seminar, 'Msonkihano wa Kakonzedwe ka Zitukuko Mudela Lathu,'" draft procedures to the IRDP/EP, January 1991.

"The Ward Planning Event," draft procedures to the IRDP/EP, January 1991.

"Agriculture Research and Seed Sub-sector Report," from the first workshop of the 'Agricultural Sector Planning Programme (GRZ/Swedish University of Agricultural Sciences), Livingstone, Zambia, January 1991.

"Report on 'Advanced CMPP Facilitator Training Seminar' and the 'Preparation Meeting for the Regional CMPP Symposium,'" Kibaha, Tanzania, December 1990.

"MAP Consultancy Bureau: A Conceptual Framework and Some Practical Issues," Lusaka, November 1990.

"Regional Conference on the Promotion of Popular Participation in Rural Development Projects," draft proposal for IAS, UNZA, September 1990.

"Terms of Reference for the Assessment of Baseline Data Collection of the CMPP in Tanzania," draft, September 1990.

"CMPP Monitoring Visit, Morogoro Region," report from Tanzania, July 1990.

"CMPP Monitoring Visit, Central Region," report from Tanzania, July 1990.

"CMPP Monitoring Visit, Coast Region," report from Tanzania, June 1990.

"Reference Group Meeting in Stockholm for MAP," June 1990.

"Advanced Facilitator Training and Project Refinement Seminar for CMPP," report of Dodoma seminar, December, 1989.

"Report on CORECU CMPP (MUWA) Planning Workshop," Dar-es-Salaam, December 1989.

"Strategic Planning Workshops for Senior Management: An approach to Participatory Planning within a Professional Context," Lusaka, December 1989.

"Background Issues of Popular Participation," paper for the "Participation Forum" in Zambia, November 1989.

"ICA Asia Regional Seminar on Methodology of Members Participation in Cooperative Societies," report Dhaka, May 1989.

"Discussions about the Future Design of CMPP in Zambia," May 1989.

"Self-evaluation Discussions of CMPP in Morogoro," report, May 1989.

"Workshop Report on CRCU CMPP Planning," Dodoma, May 1989.

"Zambia National CMPP Project Discussions," report, April 1989.

"Report on the CMPP Facilitators Training Seminar in Zambia," Lusaka, January 1989.

"Seminar for Advanced Facilitator Training and Project Refinement of CMPP in Morogoro," report, December 1988.

"Manual for Advanced Facilitator Training and Project Refinement of CMPP in Morogoro," November 1988.

"Participation as a Means for Cooperative Education," a paper presented at the Annual Symposium at the Cooperative College in Moshi, Tanzania, September 1988.

"Manual for Management Committee Seminars for Prospective SCC Supported Regions," 1988.

"Report of the CMPP Study Tour in Morogoro and Ifakara, Tanzania," 1988.

"MAP Quarterly Reports," Lusaka, January 1989 - December 1990.

"CMPP Quarterly Reports," Nairobi, July 1986 - December 1989.

Hans Hedlund:

"A proposed introduction of the CMPP Participation Approach and Grassroots Planning in the Integrated Rural Development Programme (IRDP), Eastern Province," September 1989.

"A proposed Introduction of the CMPP Participation Approach and Grassroots Planning in the Integrated Rural Development Programme (IRDP), Luapula," June 1989.

"Project document and 1989 Plan of Operation for MUWA, Mpango wa Ushirikishwaji Wana Washirika, Morogoro Region, Tanzania" (draft version), April 1989.

"Draft Report on the CMPP Activities in the Luapula Province," March 1989.

"A Proposed Introduction of the CMPP Participation Approach and Grassroots Planning in the Babati Land Management Pilot Project for Environmental Conservation," September 1988.

"Prices and Fluctuations - Three Case Studies on Members' Views on Cooperative Development," 1989.

Coffee, Co-operatives and Culture: An Anthropological Study of a Coffee Co-operative in Kenya, 1992.

"Report on CMPP Work Carried-out in Tanzania, Zambia, Zimbabwe," April 1988.

Hans Hedlund and Terry Bergdall:

"Report on the Introduction of the Method for Active Participation (MAP) Village Approach in the Babati Land Management Project, Tanzania," October 1989.

"Progress Report of CMPP in Morogoro," April 1989.

"Facilitators Manual for CMPP in Tanzania," January 1989.

"Commentary on the Preliminary Report of the External Evaluation of CMPP in Morogoro," 1988.

"MAP Annual Reports," Lusaka, 1988 and 1989.

Terry Bergdall and Chama Chapeshamano:

"Evaluation of Branch Development Seminars in the Chama District," for the IRDP/EP of Zambia, June 1991.

Upali Herath:

"Cooperative Members' Participation Programme in Africa," a report of a study tour to Zambia of the International Cooperative Alliance, New Delhi, 1988.

Justina Mapulanga and Birgitta Svensson-Thackray:

"CMPP A Practical Approach to Cooperative Training: The Zambian Case," Cooperative College, December 1989.

Bilali Omari, A.:

"CMPP in Morogoro," paper prepared for the Cooperative Congress sponsored by the International Cooperative Alliance in Stockholm, 1988.

Adam Shafi and E. Danda:

"Report of the Evaluation Mission on Education and Cooperative Members' Participation Programme (CMPP) in Morogoro Region," 1988.

Birgitta Svensson:

"Report from the CMPP Facilitators Workshop held at Kafue River Motel, 13-16 November, 1988."

"Cooperative Members' Participation Programme (CMPP): Experiences of Participation," a paper prepared at the PPU Workshop on Primary Cooperative Societies and Rural Development in Luapula Province.

"Cooperative Members' Participation Programme and Society Development," a paper presented at the Society Cooperative Development Managers Seminar in Chigola.

H. Thorfinn and K. Haux:

"Video of Melela CMPP," a video document of a CMPP seminar in Morogoro, November 1988.

E. Wekwe:

"The Cooperative Members' Participation Programme: The Morogoro Experience," a paper prepared for the Annual Symposium at the Cooperative College in Moshi, September 1988.

REFERENCES

Alila, P.O., and Obaso, J.H., "Kenya National Federation of Cooperatives (KNFC) Cooperative Members' Participation Programme (CMPP) CMPP Evaluation Study," (mimeo) November 1990.

Birgegard, L-E., "People's Participation," International Rural Development Centre, Swedish University of Agricultural Sciences, Uppsala, February 1990.

Birgegard, L-E., "A Process Approach to Policy and Project Analysis with the Ambition to Reduce External (Donor/Consultant) Influence," International Rural Development Centre, Swedish University of Agricultural Sciences, Uppsala, September 1990.

Bugnicourt, J., "Popular Participation in Development in Africa," in "Assignment Children," UNICEF Journal, 58-59, 1982.

Chambers, R., **Managing Rural Development**, Scandinavian Institute of African Studies, Uppsala, 1974.

Chapeshamano, C.S., and Bergdall, T.D., "Evaluation of Branch Development Seminars in Chama District," (mimeo) Integrated Rural Development Programme, Chipata, Zambia, June 1991.

Development Studies Unit, "Guidelines for Consultations and Popular Participation in Development Processes and Projects," Department of Social Anthropology, University of Stockholm, October 1990.

Esteya, G., "Beware of Participation," in "Development: The Journal of the Society for International Development," March 1985.

Eklof, J., and Keregero, K.J.B., "Data Collection and Information Handling in the CMPP Programme, Cooperative Union of Tanzania," (mimeo) Swedish Cooperative Centre, Stockholm, May 1991.

Fones-Sundell, M., Erikson, J., and Berresford, A., "Agricultural Sector Planning Programme 1990-91: Mid-term Progress Report," (mimeo) Swedish University Agricultural Sciences, Uppsala, April 1991.

Food and Agriculture Organisation of the UN, "The People's Participation Programme in Africa," FAO Regional Office for Africa, Accra, (undated).

Freire, P., **The Pedagogy of the Oppressed**, Penguin, Middlesex, 1972.

Genberg, B., and Hedlund, H., "Towards an Analysis of the Human Development Approach of the Institute of Cultural Affairs in Kenya," (mimeo) Swedish Cooperative Centre, September, 1982.

Gikonyo, W., "Development by the People: A Case Study of the Work of the Institute of Cultural Affairs in Central Division, Machakos District, Kenya," (mimeo) November 1982.

Goransson, G., and Saasa, O.S., "Evaluation of the Cooperative Members Participation Programme in Zambia During the Pilot Phase: 1987-1989," (mimeo) September 1990.

Hedlund, H., "Recommendations Concerning the Implementation of the Cooperative Members' Participation Programme (CMPP) in Kenya," SCC, February 1986.

Hedlund, H., "Draft Report on the CMPP Activities in the Luapula Province," (mimeo) MAP R&D Project, Lusaka, March, 1989.

Huizer, G., "Guiding Principles for People's Participation Projects: Design, Operation, Monitoring and Evaluation," FAO, Rome, 1983.

Institute of Cultural Affairs International, "Annual Report 1990," Brussels, 1990.

Institute of Cultural Affairs International, "The Network Exchange," Brussels, December 1990.

International Conference on Popular Participation in the Recovery and Development Process in Africa, "African Charter for Popular Participation in Development and Transformation," (mimeo) Arusha, February 1990.

Integrated Rural Development Programme/Eastern Province, "Phasing Out the Integrated Rural Development Programme, 1991-1993," (mimeo) Chipata, January 1991.

Hope, A., and Timmel, S., Training for Transformation: A Handbook for Community Workers, Mambo Press, Gweru, Zimbabwe, 1984.

Jonsson, U., Tilakaratna, S., Keregero, K.J.B., and Lwelamila, A.J., "Planning Rural Development at Village Level: A Summary of the Project's Objectives, Methodology and Progress," (mimeo) Dar-es-Salaam, April 1987.

Kibwana, O.T., "People's Participation Programme: An Operational Manual for Tanzania," (mimeo) Cooperative College, Moshi, December 1984.

Korten, D., and Klass, R., et al., People Centred Development: Contributions Toward Theory and Planning Development, Kumarian Press, West Hartford, 1984.

LeCompte, B., Project Aid: Limitations and Alternatives, OECD, Paris, 1986.

Lombard, S., The Growth of Cooperatives in Zambia 1914-71, UNZA Institute for African Studies, Lusaka, 1971.

MacPherson, S., Social Policy in the Third World, Wheatself Books, Brighton, 1985.

McCracken, J., Pretty, J., and Conway, G., **An Introduction to Rapid Rural Appraisal for Agricultural Development**, IIED, London, 1988.

Midgley, J., Hall, A., Hardiman, M., and Nardine, D., **Community Participation, Social Development, and the State**, Methuen and Co., 1986.

Milimo, M.C., and Uitto, J.I., "Zambia Cooperative Members' participation Programme: Assessment of the Pilot Programme in Southern Province," (mimeo) SCC, September 1988.

Mattee, A.Z., "The CMPP Programme in Tanzania: Lessons from Two Monitoring Studies in the Morogoro Region," paper presented at the National CMPP Facilitators Meeting, Dar-es-Salaam, July 1991.

Mvena, Z.S.K., Rutachokozibwa, V., and Mattee, A.Z., "The First Monitoring Report of the Impact of CMPP (MUWA) in the Morogoro Regional Cooperative Support Programme," (mimeo) Department of Agricultural Education and Extension, Sokoine University of Agriculture, Morogoro, January 1989.

Noppen, D., and Fuglesang, M., "The Cooperative Members' Participation Programme (CMPP): Reflections on the Practice of a Consultation Method for Local Level Planning in Tanzania," Working Paper No. 4, Development Studies Unit, Department of Social Anthropology, University of Stockholm, Stockholm, December 1988.

Oakley, P., and Marsden, D., **Approaches to Participation in Rural Development**, International Labour Organisation, Geneva, 1984.

Oakley, P., "The Monitoring and Evaluation of Popular Participation in Development," (mimeo) UN Economic Commission for Africa, ICPP, Arusha, February 1990.

Oakley, P., et al., **Projects with People: The Practice of Participation in Rural Development**, International Labour Office, Geneva, 1991.

Oxfam, **The Field Directors' Handbook**, fourth edition, Oxford University Press, Oxford, 1988.
Parlett, M., and Hamilton, D., "Evaluation as Illumination," in Tawaney, D., **Curriculum Evaluation Today: Trends and Implications**, Schools Council Publications, Macmillan Education Ltd, London, 1976.
Patton, M.Q., **How to Use Qualitative Methods in Evaluation**, Sage Publications, Newbury Park, California, 1987.

Pendaeli, L., "The Community Development Trust Fund of Tanzania," unpublished lecture at the "Participation Forum," Arusha, 14-16 November 1989.

Rudqvist, A., "Fieldwork Methods for Consultations and Popular Participation," Working Paper No. 9, Development Studies Unit, Department of Social Anthropology, University of Stockholm, October 1990.

Rudqvist, A., "Popular Participation: Levels and Dimensions," (mimeo) Popular Participation Study Unit, Department of Social Anthropology, University of Stockholm, 1987.

Rudqvist, A., and Tobisson, E., "Participatory Data Collection, Analysis and Reporting: Kwale Water and Sanitation Project," Development Studies Unit, Department of Social Anthropology, University of Stockholm, November 1990.

Rutachokozibwa, V., Mvena, Z.S.K., and Mattee, A.Z., "The Second Monitoring Report of the Impact of CMPP (MUWA) in the Morogoro Regional Cooperative Support Programme," (mimeo) Department of Agricultural Education and Extension, Sokoine University of Agriculture, Morogoro, January 1991.

Stiefel, M., "Social Participation in Development," a discussion paper for the International Round Table on Social Participation in Development, Institute for Labour Studies, Geneva, 1987.

Stiefel, M., and Racelis, M., "The Role and Responsibilities of Government and Development and Donor Agencies," (mimeo) UN Economic Commission for Africa, ICPP, Arusha, February 1990.

Swedeforest Consulting AB, "Strategies and Organisation of Babati Land Management Programme: Report from the Joint Tanzanian-Swedish Revision Mission, January 15-27, 1990," (mimeo) March 1990.

Swedish Cooperative Centre, "Annual Report 1988-89," Stockholm, 1989.

Tilakaratna, S., "Planning Rural Development at Village Level (PRDVL) Project in Tanzania: A Review Report," (mimeo) Dar-es-Salaam, July 1987.

United Nations, "Popular Participation as a Strategy for Promoting Community Level Action and National Development," UN Department of International Economic and Social Affairs, New York, 1981.

United Nations Research Institute for Social Development, **The Quest for a Unified Approach to Development**, UNRISD, 1980.

Uphoff, N., quoted in Pearse, A., and Stiefel, M., "Debaters' Comments on 'Inquiry into Participation: A Research Proposal,'" UNRISD, Geneva, 1980.

van Heck, B., "Training of Group Promoters in Field Projects of the Peoples's Participation Programme," (mimeo) FAO, Rome, July 1983.

Verhagen, K., **Cooperation for Survival**, Royal Tropical Institute, Amsterdam, 1984.

Verhagen, K., **Self-help Promotion**, Royal Tropical Institute, Amsterdam, 1987.

Walsh, T., "Training for Transformation: Institutional Position Paper," in "Rural Development Projects and Popular Participation," edited by Saasa, O., Institute for African Studies, University of Zambia, Lusaka, 1990.

White, A., "Why Community Participation," in "Assignment Children," UNICEF Journal, 58-59, 1982.

Wisner, B., **Power and Need in Africa**, Earthscan, London, 1988.

Wolfe, M., "Participation in Economic Development," in "Assignment Children," UNICEF Journal, 58059, 1982.